PROGRAM GUIDE

Who I Can Be Is Up to Me

Lessons in Self-Exploration and Self-Determination for Students with Disabilities in Learning

Gloria D. Campbell-Whatley

Research Press 2612 North Mattis Avenue ▼ Champaign, Illinois 61822
[800] 519-2707 ▲ www.researchpress.com

Copyright © 2004 by Gloria D. Campbell-Whatley

5 4 3 2 1   04 05 06 07 08

All rights reserved. Printed in the United States of America.

In this volume, those materials accompanied by instructions that allow the reader to photocopy them may be reproduced for noncommercial use by the original purchaser only, not to extend to reproduction by other parties. Excerpts may be printed in connection with published reviews in periodicals without express permission. No other part of this book may be reproduced by any means without the written permission of the publisher.

Copies of this book may be ordered from Research Press at the address given on the title page.

Composition by Jeff Helgesen
Cover design by Linda Brown, Positive I.D. Graphic Design, Inc.
Printed by McNaughton & Gunn, Inc.

ISBN 0-87822-484-X
Library of Congress Control Number 2003098367

Contents

Acknowledgments vii
Introduction 1

LESSON 1

What Does It Mean to Have a Disability in Learning? 5

Activity 1	A Broken Arm 5
Activity 2	Types of Disabilities 6
Activity 3	On Target: Knowing and Describing My Disability to Others 6

LESSON 2

Successful People with Disabilities 13

Activity 4	Profile: Stevie Wonder 13
Activity 5	Profile: Jim Abbott 13
Activity 6	Profile: Tom Cruise 14
Activity 7	Look at What I Can Do 15
Activity 8	Just Picture It 15

LESSON 3

Characteristics Related to Disabilities in Learning 23

Activity 9	Problems Related to a Disability in Learning 24
Activity 10	Name My Characteristics 24
Activity 11	How My Disability Is Different at School, Home, and Work 25

LESSON 4

Getting into a Special Education Program 31

Activity 12	Getting Placed in a Special Education Class 31
Activity 13	Different Tests and Their Definitions 31
Activity 14	Stepping-Stones to Special Education 32

LESSON 5

Knowing My Strengths and Weaknesses   37

Activity 15   Knowing My Strengths   38
Activity 16   Knowing My Weaknesses   38
Activity 17   Helping Myself   38
Activity 18   Contents of Folder   39
Activity 19   All about Me   39

LESSON 6

Problem Scenarios and Self-Advocacy   47

Activity 20   Dealing with the Problem   47
Activity 21   Different Ways of Looking at Problems   48
Activity 22   Beverly's Problem   48
Activity 23   Teacher's Surprise Comment   48

LESSON 7

Strategies for Handling Anger   55

Activity 24   Watching My Body for Anger   55
Activity 25   What Should I Do When People Make Fun of Me?   56

LESSON 8

Dealing with My Emotions   61

Activity 26   Dealing with My Emotions   62
Activity 27   Making Me Feel Better   62

LESSON 9

Accepting Myself   67

Activity 28   Negative Messages   67
Activity 29   Understanding My Self-Talk   68
Activity 30   Self-Talk   68

LESSON 10

Making Friends and Getting Along with Others   75

Activity 31   Keys to Getting Along with Others   75
Activity 32   Situational Analysis   77

LESSON 11

Communicating with Parents   83

Activity 33   Dialoguing with Parents   83
Activity 34   Guidelines and Sample Schedule   84
Activity 35   Schedule Form   84

LESSON 12

Responsibility Basics   91

Activity 36   Responsibility   91
Activity 37   Responsible or Irresponsible?   92

LESSON 13

Paying Attention, Focusing, and Organizing   97

Activity 38   Strategies to Strengthen Focusing Skills   97
Activity 39   Strategies to Strengthen Organizational Skills   97
Activity 40   Strategies to Strengthen My Skills   97
Activity 41   Scheduling Tasks   98

LESSON 14

Rejecting Discrimination   105

Activity 42   Discriminatory Statements   106

LESSON 15

Getting a Job   111

Activity 43   Sample Job Application   114
Activity 44   Preparing a Résumé   114
Activity 45   Sample Interview Questions: How Would You Answer These?   114
Activity 46   Dressing Appropriately   114
Activity 47   Good Job Skills   114

References and Resources   123
About the Author   127

Acknowledgments

I want to acknowledge my family for their love and support through this endeavor: Christian Campbell Whatley, my daughter, and my sisters Dr. Myrtle V. Campbell and Dr. DeSilver Cohen. I would also like to pay homage to the deceased members of my family: Jerry Campbell, my brother, and Evelyn and Jonathan Campbell, my parents. I wish to thank my friends Beverly Mitchell and Raejeanne Butler as well as Victure Scruggs, Michelle Gamble Wesley, and Janice Houston Johnson, who have listened intently to my many concerns and provided encouragement at all times.

Introduction

How exciting it is when people find that they are able to determine their path in life by exploring their innermost wants and needs, likes and dislikes, and strengths and weaknesses. Trouble is, not everyone is blessed with the ability to engage in self-exploration and self-determination.

For people with disabilities in learning—especially young people—understanding their strengths and weaknesses and their capabilities and limitations is something they have to work at. From our experience as special education teachers, we know they need help with self-exploration; it's just a matter of figuring out how we can best help them to comprehend the importance of getting to know themselves better. These students have so many questions and so few answers. They want to get from point A to point Z, but they don't know how to do it. They want to take control of their lives, but they typically don't feel that they can achieve that goal. They need our guidance so they can experience the joy of unlocking their potential.

For a number of reasons, it's not surprising that many special education students are in the dark when it comes to finding their way. After all, how can students with disabilities in learning be taught to exhibit self-regulated and goal-directed behaviors if they don't have a clear idea of what they are capable and incapable of accomplishing? How can they know their strengths and weaknesses if they have not really dug deep into the world of self-exploration? Of supreme importance to these students is finding the answer to a knotty question: How can they assimilate into school and society and determine their own course in life?

Research in this area has shown a link between self-exploration and self-determination. According to Wehmeyer, Argan, and Hughes (2000), self-determined people exhibit control over their lives by responding to events in an independent, empowered, self-realized manner. Field, Martin, Miller, Ward, and Wehmeyer (1998) hold that it is essential for self-determined people to understand their strengths and limitations and become aware of heretofore unexplored capabilities that have lain dormant for years.

For students with disabilities in learning, the concept of self-determination may seem fuzzy. For special education instructors, teaching students to master—or at least try to master—the art of self-determination is a clearly defined goal. There is nothing at all fuzzy about it.

The merits of self-determination have been discussed in recent studies (Argan, Snow, & Swaner, 1999; German, Martin, Marshall, & Sale,

2000). These studies indicate that students who are taught strategies germane to self-determination learn to serve as their own support systems and thus achieve greater control over their choices, behaviors, and lives in general. Wehmeyer and Schwartz (1997), in an assessment of 80 students with learning disorders, noted that students who exhibited a great many self-determined behaviors achieved better in school and also had more positive adult outcomes than students who exhibited relatively few self-determined behaviors. Gerber, Ginsberg, and Reiff (1992) found that adults with disabilities in learning who also possessed self-determined qualities had already set goals for their lives and were driven to achieve those goals.

The research (Wall & Dattilo, 1995; West, Barcus, Brooke, & Rayfield, 1995), which suggests that self-determination skills be pursued as tenaciously as any other skills taught to students with disabilities in learning, also strongly advises special educators to teach self-determination strategies systematically. According to Argan, Snow, and Swaner (1999), 77 percent of the special educators surveyed in their study considered the teaching of self-determination skills a top priority.

Who I Can Be Is Up to Me provides teachers with an easy-to-use lesson plan format for teaching self-determination strategies to students with disabilities in learning. Geared more toward students in the upper-elementary and middle school grades (specifically grades 5 through 9), the curriculum can also be adapted for use at the high school level. It addresses the advocacy needs of students by offering 15 lessons in self-knowledge and self-exploration that teachers can use to assist students in understanding and coping with their disabilities. Because many of these students are so busy focusing on day-to-day challenges that are often compounded by their disabilities, this method of teaching is advantageous; it gives them time to learn self-exploration skills without feeling pressured.

Once students get to know themselves, they will find it easier to come to terms with their strengths and weaknesses, some of which are readily apparent to them and some of which have been hiding beneath the surface. As a result, students will be better prepared not only to survive the challenges they encounter at school, home, and work, but to conquer them as well. They will also be able to explain, or describe, how it feels to have a disability that some people cannot detect. The lessons presented in this book will teach students how to describe their disabilities in learning clearly, calmly, and in a reasoned manner so that they can get the assistance they may need in various settings.

Typically, the teaching of self-advocacy, self-determination, and related curriculums has been limited to secondary students and adults with disabilities as they prepare to enter the world of work. Actually, the foundation of these skills should be laid much earlier, and instruction should continue throughout the stages of a youth's development. The progression of learning these skills should unfold as the student matures. Wehman and Kregel (1997) describe the types of skills that should be taught and at which stages of development: (a) awareness in the elementary years, (b) exploration in the middle school years,

(c) preparation in the high school years, and finally (d) job or academic placement in the postsecondary years.

Many texts focus on helping students comprehend and accept their learning disabilities. Yet, although these texts help students understand how they differ from others, they are not instructional in nature. Because students with learning difficulties need guidance, support, and encouragement to learn new ideas, a lesson plan format is an ideal way both to facilitate strategic instruction in the classroom and to convey new concepts.

How people respond to teaching and how they react to success and failure is determined by the attitudes and beliefs they have about themselves. According to Muller, Chambliss, and Muller (1983, March), because self-concept can be altered, a change in perspective can affect the general behavior and attitude of the individual. Interventions that have a positive effect on one's self-concept include activities that encourage positive self-reflection and self-references (Obiakor, Algozzine, & Campbell-Whatley, 1997).

Surveys have shown that the effectiveness of a curriculum can be measured by students' increased self-knowledge. Because students' self-knowledge is essential to a positive self-concept, students should be able to apply the skills taught in this book to their daily lives and notice improvement in their self-concept.

One of the problems facing special education students is that many of them are either unaware of various aspects of special education or have based their knowledge of special education on misinformation, misconceptions, and preconceptions, such as the following:

- No knowledge of what specific special education class they are attending

- A limited awareness that failure in school is related to their disability in learning—and the accompanying belief that they can make better grades if they simply try harder

- The belief that their parents think their academic failure is related to a lack of motivation rather than a disability in learning

- The belief that their general education teachers think their academic failure is related to a lack of motivation rather than a disability in learning

- The belief that they have no disability at all

- A lack of awareness of strategies that could assist them in the general education classroom

Who I Can Be Is Up to Me consists of this Program Guide and a Student Manual, which you will use to teach 15 lessons. As you move from lesson to lesson, your students will follow your directions, using their Student Manual to complete the activities in each lesson. (The activities in the Student Manual also appear in the Program Guide at the end of each lesson.) Depending on the age and ability level of your students, each lesson can be taught in 20- to 50-minute sessions two to four times a week. Remember, though, that each lesson is not necessarily intended to be completed in one week, although it can be. Much of your teaching strategy depends on your knowledge of your students and their needs. If you feel it necessary to spend more than a week per lesson, that's fine. In fact, modifications and variations in the procedure can prove useful because they provide reinforcement and increase skill attainment (McGinnis & Goldstein, 1997). A good practice is to reinforce students' learning by reminding students to apply the skills they have acquired to various situations, whether in the classroom or at home, work, or elsewhere. Keep in mind that you should have realistic expectations of your students' ability to remember what they have learned and to apply their knowledge to different situations. As with all students, their level of skill attainment is based on individual potential (Cartledge & Milburn, 1995).

It is crucial that you involve your students in the learning process by making sure that all of them are engaged. With this lesson plan format, that goal is relatively easy to achieve. For instance, each lesson suggests several role-play scenarios that encourage student-generated situations. Students may encounter some of these same situations outside the classroom, and so what they learn in class can prove useful after the bell rings.

Their answers to the questions on the pretests and posttests in your Program Guide will give you a good idea of how well your students are absorbing the information you are teaching them. Before each lesson, make two photocopies of the pretest/posttest that appears at the very end of each lesson. At the top right-hand corner of the page are the words *pretest/posttest*. Before you begin the actual lesson, circle or highlight the word *pretest* and then administer the test to the class. After the lesson, circle or highlight the word *posttest* and then administer that test as well. You will be able to tell how well your students are performing by comparing their answers on the five-item, yes-or-no tests. Note that the posttest should be administered to your students no longer than a week after the lesson has been presented.

Lesson 1

What Does It Mean to Have a Disability in Learning?

GOAL To help students define the various categories of disabilities and realize that not all disabilities are of a physical nature

PROCEDURE
1. Administer the pretest.

2. Have the class turn to **Activity 1—A Broken Arm—**on **page 1** of the Student Manual. Read the vignette aloud as students read along with you.

3. Ask students whether a physical disability is considered the "only true disability."

    Having heard the vignette, most students will answer no. To those who respond yes, suggest that they may want to change their minds by the end of the lesson.

4. Note that some students have trouble believing that they have a disability. Be aware that these students may become defensive about their disability.

5. Ask the class if a parent or teacher has ever said to them something like this: "You could do better if you tried harder."

    Most students will say they have heard such a comment both from parents and from teachers.

6. Ask students if they have ever had a general education teacher think the same way as the general education teacher in the vignette.

    The overwhelming majority of students will say yes and offer examples involving teachers from a variety of academic subjects, such as spelling, English, math, social studies, and science.

7. Engage the class in a question-and-answer session designed to elicit their thoughts about disabilities and their feelings when teachers criticize them for being slow learners or just plain lazy.

    Students are likely to report that they were taken by surprise by their teachers' remarks and felt distress. They may express their thoughts by commenting, "I felt embarrassed" or "I was sad, confused, and angry" or "I was unhappy" or "My feelings were hurt."

8. As you continue dialoguing with students, ask them what steps—if any—they took to soften the blow of their teachers' harshness.

   Some students will say they didn't know whether they should say anything at all. Thus they might admit, "I felt powerless, so I did nothing."

   Other students will tell you that they knew they were in the right but still could not do much more than seethe silently and hope the teacher noticed how angry they were. Therefore, a student might tell you, "I really didn't do anything except look upset and let my shoulders droop. The teacher could see that I was mad."

9. Ask the class, "Do disabilities exist that may not be readily visible or noticeable to others?"

   A likely response would be, "Yes, I think so, but I'm not sure."

10. Tell students that the answer is yes. Let them know that people with physical disabilities have difficulty getting around and that some cannot move about without the help of crutches, a wheelchair, or a prosthesis; in this case, a prosthesis would be an artifical leg.

11. Tell the class that a person with a disability in learning—just like the person with a physical disability—needs assistance.

12. Explain to students that people with disabilities in learning may not be able to learn at the same rate or in the same way as people without disabilities.

    It is at this juncture that students may realize that they themselves have a disability.

13. Direct students to **Activity 2—Types of Disabilities**—on **page 2** of the Student Manual, which lists three different types of disabilities. Use this activity as a starting point for helping students to examine their own disability.

14. Ask for a volunteer. Blindfold the student and then ask him or her either to read a passage from a book or to walk to the door without assistance.

    Once the student realizes that the request is absurd, explain that both special and general education students probably will not be able to achieve success without using some type of strategy or accommodation.

    Discuss how a person with a physical disability might use a wheelchair to assist with mobility, whereas a person who is visually impaired or blind might use Braille or books on tape to assist with reading.

    Point out that disability does not indicate failure but rather the need for additional assistance.

15. Have students describe their disability to peers or teachers by role-playing or writing a short script. **Activity 3—On Target: Knowing and Describing My Disability to Others**—on **page 3** of the Student Manual will help students learn what words to use to

describe their disability (e.g., dyslexia, difficulty with math, lack of organizational skills).

16. Continue discussing and role-playing until students are able to give a clear and accurate definition of a disability in learning.

17. Explain to students how a disability in learning might cause them difficulty in school, at home, and at work. Tell them that in later lessons they will learn strategies that will help them make accommodations for their disability in learning.

18. Discuss with the class an array of jobs they might find attractive, the skills those jobs will require, and the accommodations that students will need to make for each job.

19. Give the class a specific homework assignment, individualized for each student, and have them complete it before the next session.

20. Administer the posttest.

Activity 1   **Lesson 1**

A Broken Arm

Mary King is a special education teacher at Kirby Middle School. Helen Williams, an English teacher, is co-teaching the class. Jim, a highly motivated student with disabilities in learning, is failing English because of his poor reading and spelling skills. His work in the literature section of the class was fine because the stories were being read aloud in class.

Mary helped Jim with his spelling, but because of his reading level, he was still unable to spell most words correctly. Mary told Helen that she should allow Jim to pick a correctly spelled word from a list of three words or perhaps use the word in a sentence.

Helen believed that Jim's lessons should not be adapted. She said, "That will not work because those skills do not test spelling! He's no different than anyone else."

Mary said, "Helen, I don't think spelling is a skill that Jim will ever be able to learn well. It is simply part of his disability. If he had a broken arm, would you still expect him to write? Would you expect him to read printed material if he were blind?"

"Of course not," Helen said, "but this is not the same."

"Yes, it is," Mary said.

*Student Manual
page 2*

Activity 2 — Lesson 1

Types of Disabilities

Disabilities in learning

Needing to learn things a different way despite often being as knowledgeable as other students

Emotional disturbance

Trouble with the way you act or feel

Attention-Deficit/Hyperactivity Disorder (AD/HD)

Having difficulty focusing or organizing

Student Manual
page 3

Activity 3 **Lesson 1**

On Target:
Knowing and Describing My Disability to Others

I will use these words when I describe my disability to others: "I have a disability in learning."

"This means that _____

_____

_____

_____

_____."

"I may need your help to _____

_____

_____

_____

_____."

LESSON 1   **Pretest/Posttest**

What Does It Mean to Have a Disability in Learning?

Name _____ Date _____

Instructions: Read each sentence and check either **Yes** or **No.**

Yes	No	
❏	❏	1. I have a disability.
❏	❏	2. I know what type of disability I have.
❏	❏	3. I know the characteristics of my disability.
❏	❏	4. I can describe my disability to another person.
❏	❏	5. I know that I may need to make accommodations for my disability.
☐	☐	**Total**

LESSON 2

Successful People with Disabilities

GOAL For students to explore their life and career goals and be motivated by the successes achieved by people with disabilities

PROCEDURE
1. Review students' homework.

2. Administer the pretest.

3. Ask students to define the word *compensate*.

    Most will respond with comments such as "It means to make up for something."

4. Ask students if they know of ways to compensate for their disabilities.

    After some discussion, make sure your students understand that they can compensate for their disabilities by building on their strengths, using different accommodations, and getting help from you, their special education teacher. Some students will be aware of these strategies, whereas others will not.

5. Ask the class whether it is possible for people with disabilities to compensate enough to become famous.

    Most students will agree that it is possible because they have heard of and seen people who have achieved fame despite having disabilities.

6. Have students name some famous people whose disabilities did not hinder their drive for success.

    Students should be able to name several well-known people with disabilities. One name that might come up is Helen Keller, who was deaf and blind and still carved out a career as a well-respected lecturer and communicator. Another might be the inventor of the lightbulb, Thomas Edison, who was thought to be dimwitted as a youth and had to be schooled at home by his mother.

7. Read aloud the brief biographies of two famous people with different disabilities and encourage the class to read them as well. The first bio—**Profile: Stevie Wonder**—is **Activity 4** and can be found on **page 4** of the Student Manual. The second bio—**Profile: Jim Abbott**—is **Activity 5** and can be found on **page 5** of the Student Manual.

8. Ask students if they think it is more difficult to overcome a physical disability or a disability in learning.

   As they ponder your question, students will likely answer with more than a simple yes or no. Expect them to offer a variety of opinions and the rationale for those opinions.

9. Ask the class how they think Stevie Wonder and Jim Abbott became successful in spite of their differing physical disabilities.

   Expect students' comments to follow along the lines of "They each had a successful attitude" or "They were both determined to succeed."

10. Explain to the class that appearances may be misleading. Although students may initially believe it harder for a person to manage a physical disability than a disability in learning, that is not always the case. Supplement your statement by having students read **Activity 6—Profile: Tom Cruise**—on **page 6** of the Student Manual.

11. Ask the class how it was possible for Tom Cruise to overcome his disability in learning—in his case, dyslexia, which is a major reading problem.

    Help students to recognize the actor's determination to explore his abilities and find his strengths.

12. Ask students if they noticed any differences between the profiles of Stevie Wonder and Jim Abbott (people with physical disabilities) and the profile of Tom Cruise (a person with no physical disabilities).

    At this point, students should be able to confirm that all three people had difficulties to overcome and were therefore equally challenged.

13. Assign students the task of researching the lives of other famous people with disabilities. Ask them to prepare either an oral or a written report on one such person, and tell them they can share their report with the class at a later date. This long-term homework assignment should pique students' interest and, once completed, fill them with a sense of achievement as well.

14. Have each student assume the identity of a famous person with a disability and then role-play the various situations that person might encounter at home, school, work, or play. Ask students if they think they would have more difficulty overcoming challenges than the celebrities they chose to role-play.

    Students will likely assume that the celebrities would have handled things better, that they would have found the obstacles easier to overcome. (It is up to you to dispel this notion.)

15. Ask students to look deep inside themselves and find characteristics that could help make them successful. Having already studied the traits of several famous people, they should notice similarities between their own positive characteristics and those of the celebrities.

16. To help bolster students' self-confidence, have them turn to **Activity 7—Look at What I Can Do**—on **page 7** of the Student Manual and either write about or draw pictures of three of their unique talents and special skills. Your request will help enable students to discover their singular talents and abilities, whereas previously they may not have done so.

17. Have students turn to **Activity 8—Just Picture It**—on **page 8** of the Student Manual and ask them to draw a picture or write a paragraph that depicts the types of activities they would like to be involved with in 10 or 15 years. From there, they will begin to think about realistic career choices. (Make sure you check whether their career goals match their areas of high performance.)

    By now, students will realize that they have great potential. As a result, they will begin to explore more thoroughly their short- and long-term goals and feel more comfortable dreaming about the future.

18. Give the class a specific homework assignment, individualized for each student, and have them complete it before the next session.

19. Administer the posttest.

Student Manual
page 4

Activity 4 **Lesson 2**

Profile: Stevie Wonder

Stevie Wonder, born in 1950, is a versatile, world-renowned musician. Shortly after Stevie's birth, the doctors noticed he had a medical condition that necessitated his being placed in an incubator. Although Stevie survived his ordeal, the doctors couldn't save his eyesight; he has been blind his entire life.

Stevie grew up on the east side of Detroit and began learning to play the piano when he was only 4. He also enjoyed his toy drums and, seemingly overnight, learned to play them well. When he was 9, he started singing at church. A year later, a musician friend invited him to visit the Motown recording studio. Stevie went to the studio every day after school and became familiar with an assortment of instruments. The people at Motown loved him.

Stevie used to say, "Do it over, do it differently, do it until it can't be done any better." At age 12, he produced his first hit single record, "Fingertips." When he reached high school age, Stevie decided to attend the Michigan School for the Blind. Later he studied music composition at the University of Southern California. Stevie has written and performed many hit songs and has also won many music awards.

Student Manual
page 5

Activity 5   **Lesson 2**

Profile: Jim Abbott

Michigan native Jim Abbott, born in 1967, has always loved baseball and was a standout pitcher for the University of Michigan Wolverines. After graduation, he saw his dream come true when he made it to the major leagues and became a successful starting pitcher. Drafted by the California (now Anaheim) Angels, Jim also pitched for the New York Yankees, Chicago White Sox, and Milwaukee Brewers before retiring from the game.

The remarkable thing about Abbott's ascent to the big leagues was that he was born without a right hand. His physical disability, rare for an athlete in any sport, did not interfere with his ability to pitch—and pitch well.

Because of the artificial hand he wore as a child, Jim had to endure teasing from many of his classmates, who made fun of his prosthesis. Undeterred, Jim showed off his athletic ability by hurling a no-hitter in his first Little League game. He starred on his high school baseball team and later baffled batters and onlookers while pitching for the Wolverines. Jim's unlikely accomplishments earned him a reputation as one of the most famous baseball players in collegiate annals.

A former major league all-star, Jim was not surprised by his feats on the diamond. "I don't think of myself as having a disability," he said, "because it has not kept me from doing anything I wanted to do."

Activity 6   **Lesson 2**

Profile: Tom Cruise

Tom Cruise, born in 1962, is a famous actor who has starred in films such as *Risky Business, Top Gun, Rain Man, Mission: Impossible,* and *Vanilla Sky.* He was born in New York City to a family of six—his parents and three siblings. Tom's father was an engineer, and his mother was a teacher of children with disabilities in learning. She and all of her children were dyslexic. (In other words, they all had a major reading problem.)

Tom did fine at home, but at school he had trouble keeping up with his classmates. He seemed bright, so it's no wonder his high school classmates and teachers were surprised that he was having academic problems. It wasn't long before he was placed in special education classes.

Tom was excellent at sports, especially wrestling, baseball, and hockey. After he was injured while wrestling, he decided to try out for a school play. He landed the lead role and found that he was truly talented on stage. After high school, Tom showed up for as many acting tryouts as he could in New York. His perseverance paid off, as Tom won many leading roles and is now one of the top box-office attractions in the world.

Student Manual
page 7

Activity 7   **Lesson 2**

Look at What I Can Do

Three of My Special Skills

1. _____

2. _____

3. _____

Student Manual
page 8

Activity 8 **Lesson 2**

Just Picture It

Draw a picture

Write a paragraph

_____
_____
_____
_____
_____

LESSON 2 ***Pretest/Posttest***

Successful People with Disabilities

Name _____ Date _____

Instructions: Read each sentence and check either **Yes** or **No.**

Yes No

❏ ❏   1. I can name two famous people who have disabilities.

❏ ❏   2. I know what the word *compensate* means.

❏ ❏   3. I know the things I do well.

❏ ❏   4. I kow what skills I need to strengthen to overcome my disability.

❏ ❏   5. I have goals for myself.

☐ ☐   **Total**

Lesson 3

Characteristics Related to Disabilities in Learning

GOAL To familiarize students with the characteristics of their disability so they understand why it is difficult for them to achieve in school

PROCEDURE
1. Review students' homework.

2. Administer the pretest.

3. Explain to the class that some children show signs of learning problems even before they begin their schooling. Tell students also that these children's parents possibly had learning problems back when they were starting school.

4. Ask students whether anyone in their family ever had difficulty in school.

   Some students will answer yes and talk about family members who have had difficulty with reading or math or spelling.

   Other students will name family members who have various types of physical disabilities.

5. Ask students if they were ever told that they had problems at birth.

   Answers will vary: Some students may say their parents told them that they were in an accident or had been dropped, whereas others will talk about being born with a condition that may have contributed to their disability.

6. Explain to students that they may have certain negative experiences and encounters in school. Some of them are listed here:

   Your teachers may not understand why you, unlike most other students, are unable to complete your assignments.

   You might get into more trouble than other students.

   Your brain works differently from the brains of other students. Although the brain carries messages from one's ears and eyes, your brain may not be able to carry those messages very efficiently. As a result, you may have difficulty listening, paying attention, communicating effectively, or learning certain skills such as reading or spelling or solving math problems.

7. Direct students to **Activity 9—Problems Related to a Disability in Learning—**on **page 9** of the Student Manual, which describes categories of problems associated with a disability in learning. Read aloud the brief anecdotes from each category as students follow along. This activity will introduce students to problems linked with a disability in learning and also make it easier for them to spot their own problems.

8. Have students turn to **Activity 10—Name My Characteristics—** on **page 10** of the Student Manual and have them list (a) positive and negative characteristics that they believe might be related to their disability and (b) positive and negative characteristics that are not related to their disability.

   With regard to characteristics that are not related to a disability in learning, students may be aware of a number of their negative characteristics but unaware of their many positive characteristics. They will often need help in identifying their positive characteristics. In time, students will be able to list an assortment of positive characteristics they possess that are not related to their disability, such as athletic skills, mechanical aptitudes, and cooking expertise.

   Students also will appreciate any help you can give them in identifying positive characteristics that are related to their disability—just as they will whenever you give them leeway in completing their assignments and achieving their goals. Teachers may assist students in a number of ways: allowing students extra time to complete a task, giving them permission to take oral exams rather than written tests, or working with them to shorten or otherwise modify homework assignments that may initially strike them as daunting. Negative characteristics associated with a disability in learning would include poor academic skills. Just as before, the teacher should assist the students—this time helping them identify their negative characteristics.

9. Have students role-play situations outside of school (e.g., at home or at work). During each situation they role-play—and in each environment—students should be able to explain clearly how their disability will affect them.

10. In a simulation to be played out in the classroom through role play, have students describe the characteristics of their disability to a general education teacher. (To help students learn to communicate calmly and clearly with an adult, you should pretend to be the general education teacher.)

    By this time, students should be able to define their disability clearly and to describe its characteristics as well. If they cannot, have them review the characteristics periodically.

11. As a test of students' ability to transfer to non-classroom situations the knowledge they have acquired in the classroom, have them think about how their disability may affect them in other areas of their lives and in a range of social situations.

12. Have students turn to **Activity 11—How My Disability Is Different at School, Home, and Work**—on **page 11** of the Student Manual and ask them to list the various ways their disability affects them in the three different environments. Typical responses include the following:

    At school: problems with academic subjects such as spelling and math; difficulties with writing, listening, asking questions, understanding and completing homework assignments; fear of embarrassment when their friends find out about their disability; inability to conquer behavioral problems

    At home: problems communicating with parents and siblings; uncertainty about handling social obligations; self-consciousness about their disability when in the company of relatives such as aunts, uncles, and cousins; fear of not "fitting in" with their peers in the community

    At work: problems communicating with employer, employees, and customers; difficulty performing the assigned tasks; lack of organizational skills

13. Give the class a specific homework assignment, individualized for each student, and have them complete it before the next session.

14. Administer the posttest.

Student Manual
page 9

Activity 9   Lesson 3

Problems Related to a Disability in Learning

Communication (Language Disorder)
It was hard to understand what Barbara was saying. She had to explain herself repeatedly. Sometimes the teacher had to explain instructions over and over again because Barbara could not understand what the teacher was saying.

Academics (Problems with School Work)
Rashard rarely had any of his homework completed, and he almost always turned his papers in late. He said he could not understand the math problems.

Concentration (Attention Disorder)
Mark often got in trouble because he would look out the window when the teacher was talking.

Physical Motion (Motor Disability)
Melissa got bad grades because the teacher could not read or understand her writing. She also had a lot of trouble spelling.

Friendships (Social Skills Deficits)
Philip said, "I try to make friends, but it seems like I say the wrong things to people."

Student Manual
page 10

Activity 10   **Lesson 3**

Name My Characteristics

Characteristics Not Related to a Disability in Learning		Characteristics Related to a Disability in Learning	
Positive	Negative	Positive	Negative
1. _____	_____	1. _____	_____
2. _____	_____	2. _____	_____
3. _____	_____	3. _____	_____
4. _____	_____	4. _____	_____
5. _____	_____	5. _____	_____
6. _____	_____	6. _____	_____
7. _____	_____	7. _____	_____
8. _____	_____	8. _____	_____
9. _____	_____	9. _____	_____
10. _____	_____	10. _____	_____

Lesson 3 • Characteristics Related to Disabilities in Learning

Student Manual
page 11

Activity 11 • **Lesson 3**

How My Disability Is Different at School, Home, and Work

School	Home	Work
1. _____	1. _____	1. _____
2. _____	2. _____	2. _____
3. _____	3. _____	3. _____
4. _____	4. _____	4. _____
5. _____	5. _____	5. _____

LESSON 3   **Pretest/Posttest**

Characteristics Related to Disabilities in Learning

Name _____ Date _____

Instructions: Read each sentence and check either **Yes** or **No.**

Yes   **No**

❑   ❑   1. I can name positive characteristics related to my disability.

❑   ❑   2. I can name negative characteristics related to my disability.

❑   ❑   3. I can name a number of academic areas that are affected by my disability in learning.

❑   ❑   4. I can describe how my disability affects me differently at home, school, and work.

❑   ❑   5. I know which academic areas give me the least trouble.

☐   ☐   **Total**

LESSON 4

Getting into a Special Education Program

GOAL For students to explore and understand the testing and placement procedures and eligibility requirements for special education programs

PROCEDURE
1. Review students' homework.

2. Administer the pretest.

3. Ask the class the following two questions: (a) Do you understand why you are in a special education class? (b) Do you know how you were placed in a special education class?

    Some students will be aware that they are in a special education class, whereas others will not.

    Few students will understand the procedures involved in placing students in special education classes until you explain them.

    Some students will know they are in a different class from most kids in the school, but they may not understand the nature of the class and why they have been placed there.

4. Have students turn to **Activity 12—Getting Placed in a Special Education Class**—on **page 12** of the Student Manual. Read the vignette aloud as students follow along. Make sure that students note the five steps that must be taken for them to be placed in a special education class.

    Although many students may have heard or seen the initials "IEP," they probably did not know the meaning and purpose of the IEP until reading the vignette.

5. Ask students to turn to **Activity 13—Different Tests and Their Definitions**—on **page 13** of the Student Manual. The activity describes three different types of tests used to measure certain abilities and disabilities.

6. Inform students that each of them has been placed in the special education class for a specific reason. In other words, not everyone in the class has the same disability.

    Some students will be aware of this, whereas others will not.

7. Have students look at **Activity 14—Stepping-Stones to Special Education**—on **page 14** of the Student Manual. Select two students at random and ask one of them to pretend to be a parent. Have the mock parent ask the other student questions about his or her disability. Next, have the student explain in a role play how the disability was identified and what type of testing procedure the student followed prior to being placed in the special education class.

   Depending on their age, students will have varying degrees of difficulty with this role play. At times, they may depend on verbal cues to help them with the role play.

8. Following the role play, ask the class how they might communicate the same information to a real-life peer or teacher rather than a pretend parent.

9. Ask students to discuss how they felt as they went through the testing process to determine the need for their placement in the special education class.

   Although some students will be able to name the test (or tests) they were given, they may not recall their feelings while being tested.

   Other students may recall expressing feelings of failure during the testing.

   Most students will be familiar with the three different tests described in **Activity 13.**

   A number of students may recall the disability for which they were being tested. A couple of examples of disabilities they may have been tested for are Attention-Deficit/Hyperactivity Disorder (AD/HD) or a reading disability.

   Some students will be able to remember their IQ test score.

10. Ask the class to pretend they are applying for an after-school job at a pet store and that the following situation pertains to them: They know they will need to feed the pets, but they have a disability in reading and are afraid that because they won't be able to read the pet food labels, they may harm the animals. They also fear that if they note their disability on their application, they may not get the job. How might students explain their disability to their prospective employer so that they will still be considered for the job?

    Students will suggest using various methods to explain their disability. Some students will reply that they would discuss as calmly as possible with the prospective employer the accommodations needed if they were to get the job. For example, to compensate for their difficulty in reading, perhaps the students could use a code to identify pet food labels and understand the instructions on the package.

11. Give the class a specific homework assignment, individualized for each student, and have them complete it before the next session.

12. Administer the posttest.

Student Manual
page 12

Activity 12   **Lesson 4**

Getting Placed in a Special Education Class

When Tanya was in the first grade, her teacher noticed that she had difficulty reading (Step 1).

The teacher tried different approaches to help Tanya improve her reading skills but none of her methods met with success. At that point, the teacher decided that Tanya should be tested to see whether she would do better in a special education environment (Step 2).

Before Tanya could be tested, her parents needed to sign a permission slip, which they did (Step 3).

After Tanya was tested, a group of educators—a team, actually—looked at her test scores and decided that Tanya did in fact need to be in a special education class (Step 4).

Once Tanya was placed in the class, her special education teacher wrote Tanya an Individualized Education Plan (IEP). The IEP listed what Tanya was to learn and described how she would learn it (Step 5).

Student Manual
page 13

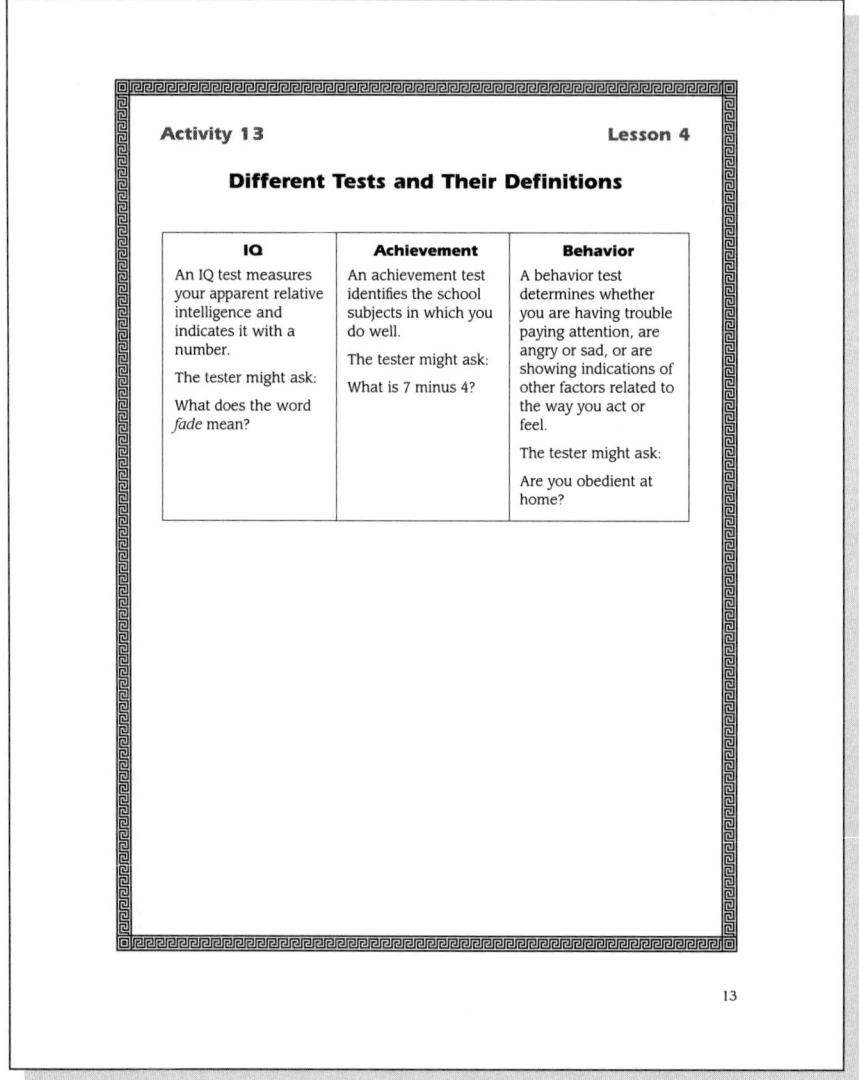

Activity 13   **Lesson 4**

Different Tests and Their Definitions

IQ	Achievement	Behavior
An IQ test measures your apparent relative intelligence and indicates it with a number. The tester might ask: What does the word *fade* mean?	An achievement test identifies the school subjects in which you do well. The tester might ask: What is 7 minus 4?	A behavior test determines whether you are having trouble paying attention, are angry or sad, or are showing indications of other factors related to the way you act or feel. The tester might ask: Are you obedient at home?

Student Manual
page 14

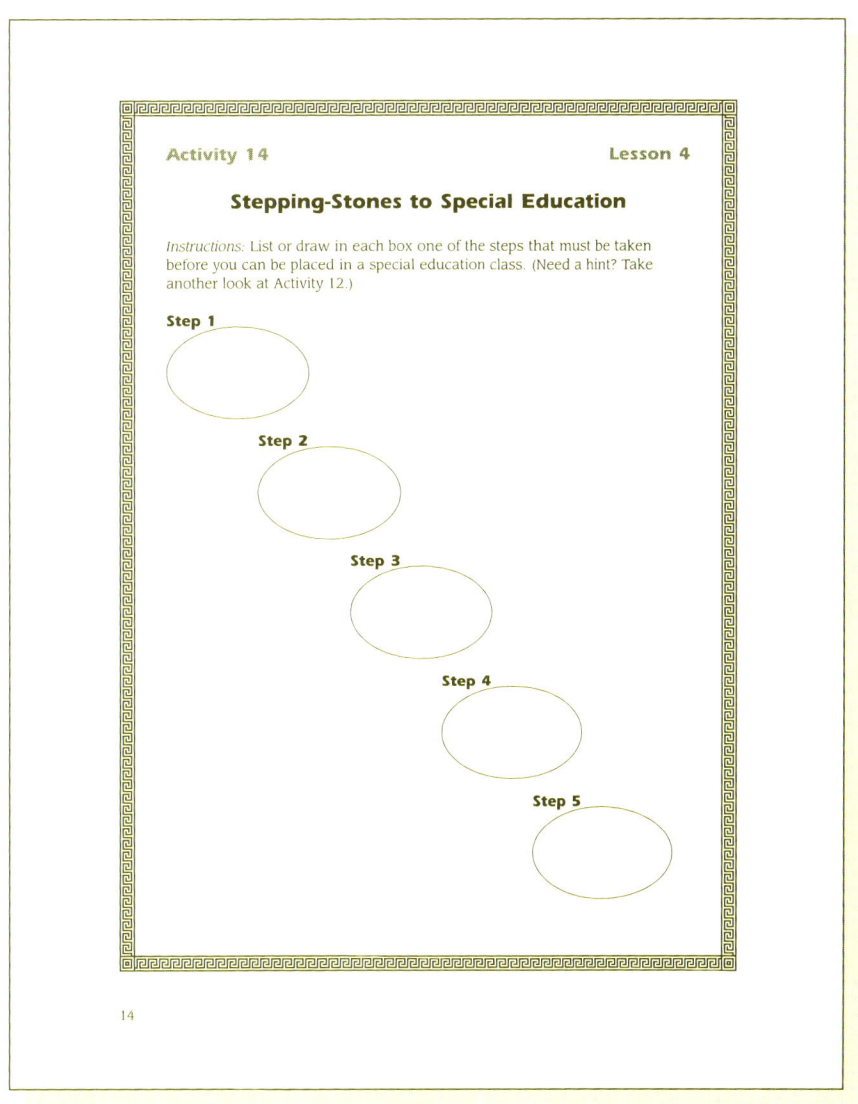

Lesson 4 • Getting into a Special Education Program

LESSON 4   **Pretest/Posttest**

Getting into a Special Education Program

Name _____ Date _____

Instructions: Read each sentence and check either **Yes** or **No**.

Yes   **No**

❏ ❏   1. I can explain the procedures for being placed in a special education program.

❏ ❏   2. I know what kind of tests I took to be placed in a special education class.

❏ ❏   3. I know why I was placed in a special education class.

❏ ❏   4. I know what it feels like to be tested for special education.

❏ ❏   5. I know what IEP means.

☐ ☐   **Total**

Who I Can Be Is Up to Me: Lessons In Self-Exploration and Self-Determination for Students with Disabilities in Learning (Program Guide)
© 2004 by Gloria D. Campbell-Whatley. Champaign, IL: Research Press. (800-519-2707)

LESSON 5

Knowing My Strengths and Weaknesses

GOAL To help students understand their strengths and weaknesses so that they can improve in these areas

PROCEDURE
1. Review students' homework.

2. Administer the pretest.

3. Engage the class in a discussion about strengths and weaknesses. Ask them the following questions:

    What is a strength?

    What is a weakness?

    Does everyone have strengths and weaknesses?

4. As students mull these questions, help spur discussion by reading aloud the following statements, which show how strengths and weaknesses vary from person to person:

    Student A may do well in math class but have difficulty in English class.

    Student B may excel in sports but not do well in social studies.

5. To enhance discussion, ask students to think of their own examples.

6. Ask students why it is important for them to understand both their strengths and their weaknesses.

7. After giving students more time to discuss, explain that knowing your strengths and weaknesses lets you build on your strengths and improve in your weak areas.

8. Emphasize that a weakness does not indicate failure, but rather an area that needs special attention.

9. Ask students whether a strength can also be a weakness.

    To increase student involvement and enthusiasm, read them an example of a strength in one area that might prove to be a weakness in a different area. (Example: Since he began lifting weights, David has built up his muscles enough to play on the football team.

Unfortunately, he is too bulked up for baseball; as a result, he has difficulty getting around on his swing.)

Encourage students to think of more examples.

10. Point out that we all need special help in our weak areas:

    If you're falling behind in math class, you may need a tutor.

    If you have difficulty reading the items on a test, you may need more time to complete the test.

    If you have trouble getting along with other students, you may need help with social skills.

11. Have students turn to **Activity 15—Knowing My Strengths—**on **page 15** of the Student Manual and ask them to list their strengths at school, home, and work. Urge them to list as many different types of strengths as they can.

12. Ask the class to complete **Activity 16—Knowing My Weaknesses—**on **page 16** of the Student Manual. The activity calls for students to list their weaknesses at school, home, and work.

13. Have students discuss the strengths and weaknesses that they listed in the two activities. Students will discover that they share many of the same traits.

14. Discuss various strategies and modifications that will assist students in maintaining their strengths and accommodating or overcoming their weaknesses.

15. Refer students to **Activity 17—Helping Myself—**on **page 17** of the Student Manual, which offers ways to improve on their weaknesses. Have them (a) check the type of help they would like to have, (b) jot down additional types of help they might need, and (c) list the names of people whom they believe can help them. Circulate among the students and be ready to coach those who are having difficulty completing this activity.

16. Read the following scenario to the class:

    Mandy is having difficulty finishing her math test. She knows how to complete the problems using TouchMath, and so she needs the number strip with the touch points. Unfortunately, her math teacher has instructed the students to clear their desks of everything besides the test. What can Mandy do?

17. Have the class discuss Mandy's problem.

    If the students are stumped, point out that Mandy can explain the TouchMath method to the math teacher and show him that her use of the number strip with the touch points is not an attempt to cheat, but rather a way of compensating for her disability in learning.

    Another possibility is for Mandy to ask her special education teacher to explain to her math teacher that the TouchMath method is used as an accommodation for students with disabilities in learning.

18. Ask students to discuss how their strengths and weaknesses are related to outcomes at school, home, and work. Explain as follows:

    A student who tries to follow directions and asks questions when he doesn't understand will probably do better with class work as well as chores at home.

    A student who is often late may have to hurry through an assignment in class and consequently earn a failing grade. She also may have trouble keeping a job.

19. Have students compile a list of personal accomplishments. **Activity 18—Contents of Folder**—on **page 18** of the Student Manual gives examples of the types of items that can be included on the list. As a homework assignment, ask students to gather three items to be placed in a folder. They can write the names of these items on **Activity 19—All about Me**—on **page 19** of the Student Manual. If they choose to, they can instead draw pictures that represent their favorite accomplishments.

20. Give the class a specific homework assignment, individualized for each student, and have them complete it before the next session.

21. Administer the posttest.

Student Manual
page 15

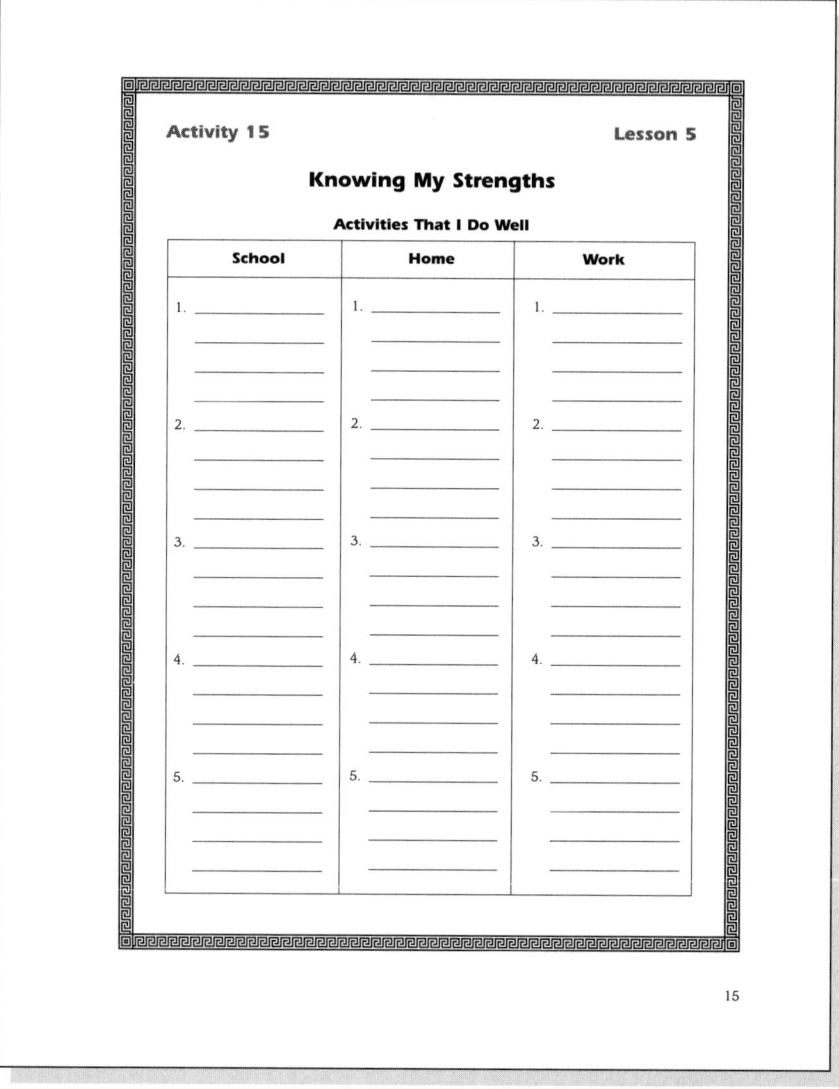

Student Manual
page 16

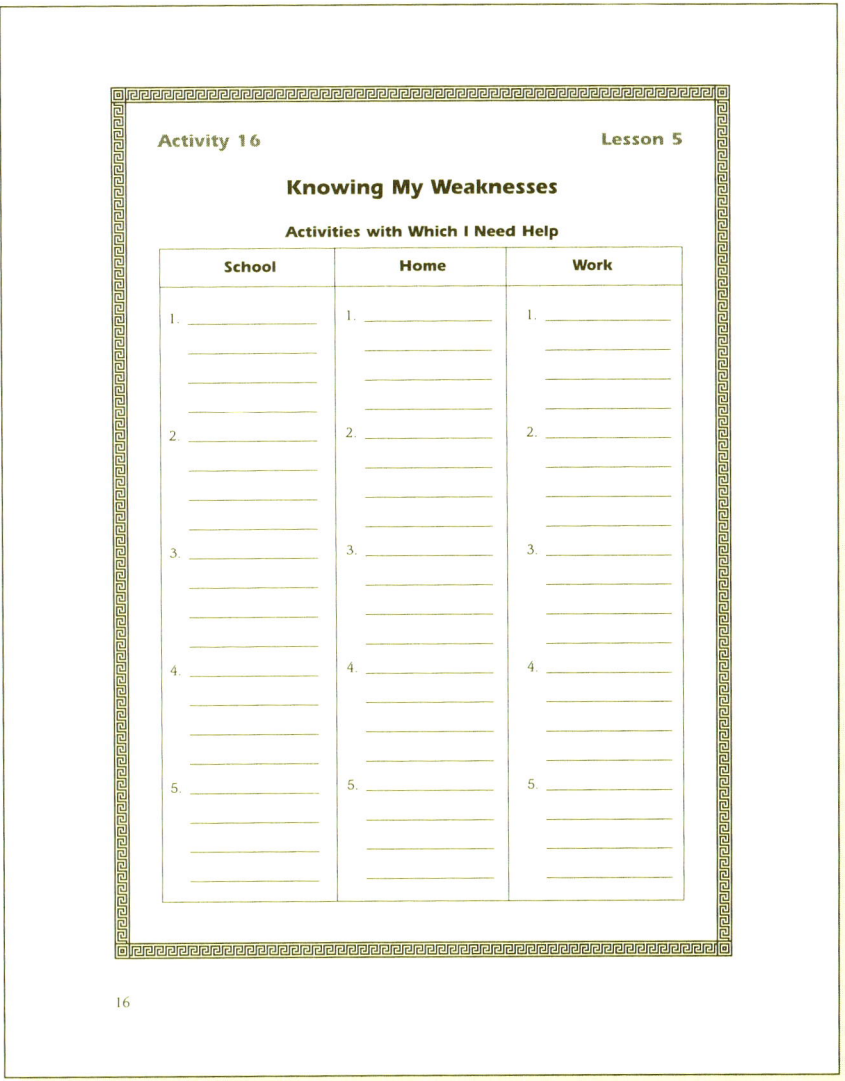

Lesson 5 • Knowing My Strengths and Weaknesses

Student Manual
page 17

Activity 17   **Lesson 5**

Helping Myself

Check any of the following that could be helpful to you.

____ Use graph paper for math problems.

____ Ask the teacher if I can have permission to do only half the problems.

____ Use a timer to help me keep my attention focused.

____ Learn how to type and use the computer rather than write assignments on paper.

____ Ask the teacher for more time to complete the assignment.

List additional types of help you may need.

_____

_____

_____

_____

_____

_____

List people whom you believe can help you.

_____

_____

_____

_____

_____

_____

_____

Student Manual
page 18

Activity 18 **Lesson 5**

Contents of Folder

Here are some examples:

Report from a hands-on lesson

Science or History Fair project

Computer-generated examples of work

Best performance

Favorite performance

Tape of performance

Learning progress record

Photographs

Awards

Personal goals

Lesson 5 • Knowing My Strengths and Weaknesses

Student Manual
page 19

Activity 19   **Lesson 5**

All about Me

Record in words or pictures your favorite accomplishments.

Words

1. _____
   _____
   _____

2. _____
   _____
   _____

3. _____
   _____
   _____

Pictures

1. [ ]   2. [ ]   3. [ ]

LESSON 5   **Pretest/Posttest**

Knowing My Strengths and Weaknesses

Name _____ Date _____

Instructions: Read each sentence and check either **Yes** or **No.**

Yes **No**

❑ ❑   1. I can name my strengths.

❑ ❑   2. I can name my weaknesses.

❑ ❑   3. I know what modification means.

❑ ❑   4. I know strategies that I can use to help me academically.

❑ ❑   5. I am able to place in a folder three items that show my strengths.

☐ ☐   **Total**

LESSON 6

Problem Scenarios and Self-Advocacy

GOAL To teach students how to behave appropriately and advocate for themselves in problem situations related to their disability

PROCEDURE
1. Review students' homework.

2. Administer the pretest.

3. Explain to students that they will occasionally be confronted with situations and problems that are related specifically to their disability. Spark discussion by asking students the following:

    Because you have a disability, do you feel helpless when others question the nature of your disability or make fun of you?

    If you do not feel helpless, what types of responses might you give?

4. Have the class share responses they have given in the past. Most students will be able to come up with recent examples of situations that occurred at school or at home.

5. Inform students that, when confronted with others' queries or taunts, they can respond in a number of ways. Explain that some responses are positive and some are negative.

6. Emphasize to students the importance of making the right (or positive) choice when responding to others.

7. Give students confidence by assuring them that they are active participants who can learn appropriate behavior and coping skills and become strong self-advocates.

    By this time, students will become aware of their capability to act on a problem rather than having the problem act on them.

8. Have students turn to **Activity 20—Dealing with the Problem—**on **page 20** of the Student Manual. Read aloud the brief scenario while the students follow along, and then ask them how they would respond to Robert's taunting of Michael.

    Because most students have encountered similar situations, some of their recollections may spark angry replies, such as "I'd hit him" or "I'd curse him."

    Other students will present positive solutions to the problem. They may say that they would simply ignore Robert or walk away, or that they might even tell him: "Yes, I am in special education, and that is OK; I need the extra help to succeed."

9. Tell students that in cases such as this, they should not let the offender see that they are angry or upset. Point out that an angry response gives the offender power over them.

10. Have students role-play similar situations so they can get a feel for what it's like to be harassed and be ready to respond appropriately.

11. Tell students that their responses to Robert's teasing of Michael are examples of assertive, nonassertive, and aggressive behaviors.

12. Have students turn to **Activity 21** on **page 21** of the Student Manual—**Different Ways of Looking at Problems**—and give them time to become familiar with the terms listed on the page. By understanding these words, students should be able to match one or more of them with their earlier responses to the problem posed in **Activity 20.**

13. As students think about the activity and their feelings, steer them away from responses that are angry or inappropriate (i.e., aggressive or nonassertive) and toward responses that are positive (i.e., assertive).

14. Remind the class that it is up to them to decide whether their solution is appropriate. Tell them that they must weigh the positives and negatives of each solution.

15. Have students turn to **Activity 22—Beverly's Problem**—and **Activity 23—Teacher's Surprise Comment**—on **pages 22** and **23,** respectively, of the Student Manual. As the class follows along, read each vignette aloud and then ask students to ponder the ramifications of each problem and write a solution they think would be appropriate.

16. Ask for volunteers or, if necessary, select students to role-play the two scenarios. Have the role players exhibit assertive, nonassertive, and aggressive behaviors. Ask them to discuss which behaviors are being displayed in each role-play situation.

17. Point out to the class that a positive solution to the problem presented in **Activity 22** would be for Beverly to describe her disability to her employer. Explain that by doing so, Beverly might achieve two goals: (a) to refute any preconceived negative notions the employer may have about people with even mild learning disabilities and (b) to present herself in a positive light that will keep her in good stead with her employer, who should be impressed with Beverly's honesty.

18. As for the scenario in **Activity 23,** suggest to the class that a good solution would be to discuss the problem with their special education teacher, who would be willing and able to dissuade the general education teacher from holding negative views of students with disabilities in learning.

19. As a homework assignment, ask students to show how they used assertive (i.e., positive) behaviors in one or more problem situations at home.

20. Administer the posttest.

Student Manual
page 20

Activity 20 **Lesson 6**

Dealing with the Problem

Robert often whispers "special education" in Michael's ear. Michael is offended and bothered. What should he do?

_____

Student Manual
page 21

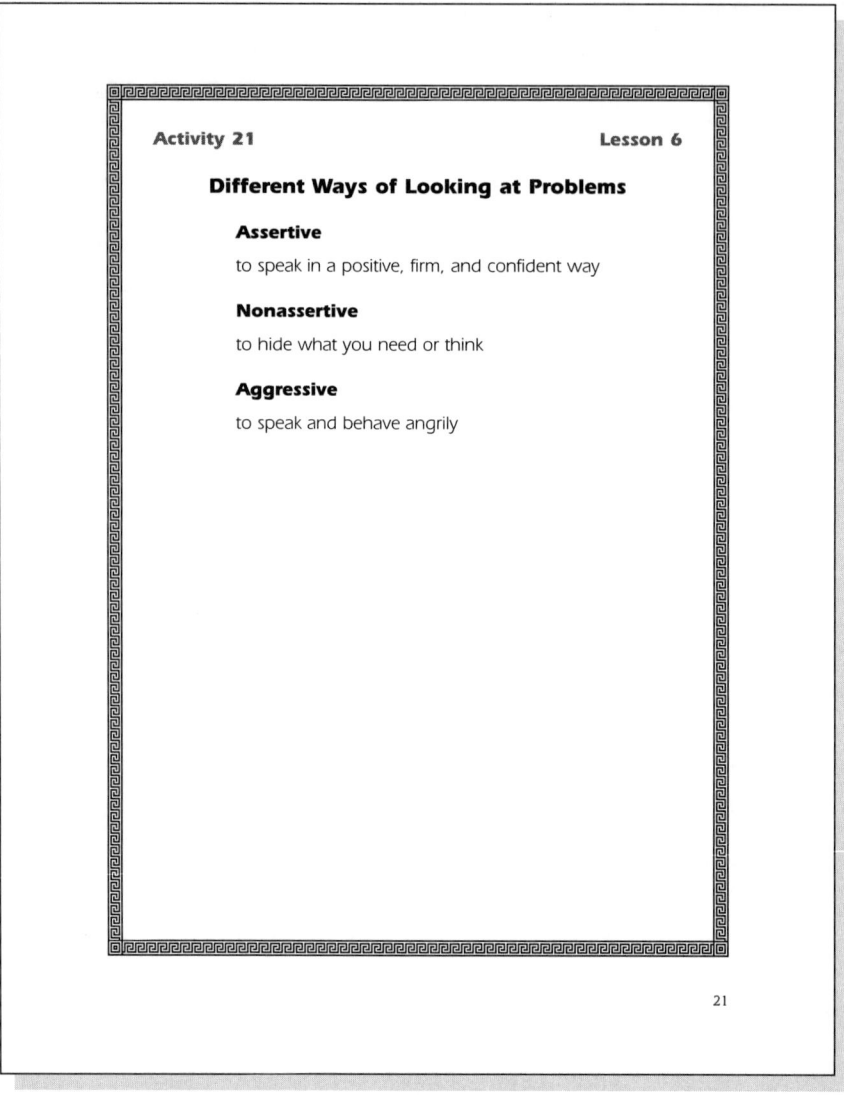

Activity 21   Lesson 6

Different Ways of Looking at Problems

Assertive

to speak in a positive, firm, and confident way

Nonassertive

to hide what you need or think

Aggressive

to speak and behave angrily

Student Manual
page 22

Activity 22 **Lesson 6**

Beverly's Problem

Beverly is going for a job interview for a part-time job after school in a store. The store manager is a friend of her mother's. Although her mother did not encourage her to take the job, Beverly is determined to make some extra cash after school to buy some things she has been wanting. Beverly is worried because her mother told the store manager that she has a mild disability. Beverly is afraid that the manager will think she cannot do the job. Should she explain that she has a mild disability before the manager mentions it?

_____

_____

_____

_____

_____

_____

_____

_____

_____

_____

_____

_____

_____

_____

Student Manual
page 23

Activity 23   **Lesson 6**

Teacher's Surprise Comment

The general education English teacher is explaining an assignment. Before finishing, she adds, "All students will have to do the assignment the same way. No one is getting out of this one." Should you as a student with a disability in learning confront the teacher about the comment? What should you do?

_____

_____

_____

_____

_____

_____

_____

_____

_____

_____

_____

_____

_____

LESSON 6   **Pretest/Posttest**

Problem Scenarios and Self-Advocacy

Name _____ Date _____

Instructions: Read each sentence and check either **Yes** or **No.**

Yes   **No**

- ❏   ❏   1. I know how to handle a situation in a positive way when someone calls me a name.

- ❏   ❏   2. I know the meaning of assertive behavior.

- ❏   ❏   3. I know the meaning of aggressive behavior.

- ❏   ❏   4. I know the meaning of nonassertive behavior.

- ❏   ❏   5. I know how to handle a situation in a positive way when a teacher is negative to me.

  ☐   ☐   **Total**

Lesson 7

Strategies for Handling Anger

GOAL To help students learn problem-solving strategies for handling anger

PROCEDURE
1. Review students' homework.

2. Administer the pretest.

3. Explain to students that anger is a normal emotion that everybody experiences. Emphasize that there are appropriate and inappropriate ways of handling anger.

4. Begin a class discussion by having students share events and experiences that have angered them.

    Some students may recall incidents in which they were angry at friends or family for a variety of reasons.

    Some may express anger at themselves for doing poorly in school.

    Some will say they have been angered by classmates who made fun of them because of their disabilities.

    Some may also express anger at certain general education teachers who have been both confrontational and insensitive to them and their disabilities.

5. Ask students how they responded to these situations.

    Answers will vary, of course, but some students will say they responded by screaming and fighting.

6. Ask the students who flew off the handle what happened as a result of their expression of anger.

    Most will say that their anger was answered with more anger from their adversary and that the experience was entirely negative.

7. Encourage students to use positive problem-solving responses, such as reasoning with the other person and talking through the problem situation. Remind the class that everyone responds differently to anger; therefore, the students' problem-solving strategies will vary from situation to situation.

8. Have the class turn to **Activity 24—Watching My Body for Anger**—on **page 24** of the Student Manual and then ask them the following questions: (a) Are you aware of how you respond to anger?

(b) How can you tell when you are becoming angry? (c) How do you feel when you are angry?

Students will likely mention obvious physical changes they notice, such as sweating, flushing, and increased heart rate.

A number of students will report reactive behaviors, such as shouting, hitting, and cursing.

9. Ask the class the following: What calms you down when you are angry?

   Students will likely answer, "Talking about the situation calmly" or "Counting to 10" or "Being alone and quiet for a while."

10. Explain to students that because of their disability in learning, they may be considered different by many general education students and often teased by them.

11. Have the class think of instances in which they were called names or teased about their disability. Ask them what they do when someone teases them.

    Typical student responses are "I shout at them" or "I hit them" or "I ignore them."

12. Ask students how they feel when they are teased: Sad? Hurt? Angry? To help them sort out their emotions, have them turn to **Activity 25—What Should I Do When People Make Fun of Me?—on page 25** of the Student Manual. Ask students to write in the third column what they would do or say. This activity will give them a good idea of the consequences of their actions when they choose a specific strategy for defusing their anger.

13. As students are mulling over their choices of response, ask them to think about how they would react in the following scenario:

    You are in a general education class and have a question about the assignment your teacher has just given. Behind you, a student whispers, "Shut up. Everyone knows the answer to that." What will you do?

14. Have students consider this and other role-play situations related to anger, including real-life situations that they have already encountered during the past week in school or at home or work.

15. Ask students to share with the class their strategy for handling their response. Because their choice of strategies may not work, have them reassess the situation and talk about what they should have done.

16. Give the class a specific homework assignment, individualized for each student, and have them complete it before the next session.

17. Administer the posttest.

Student Manual
page 24

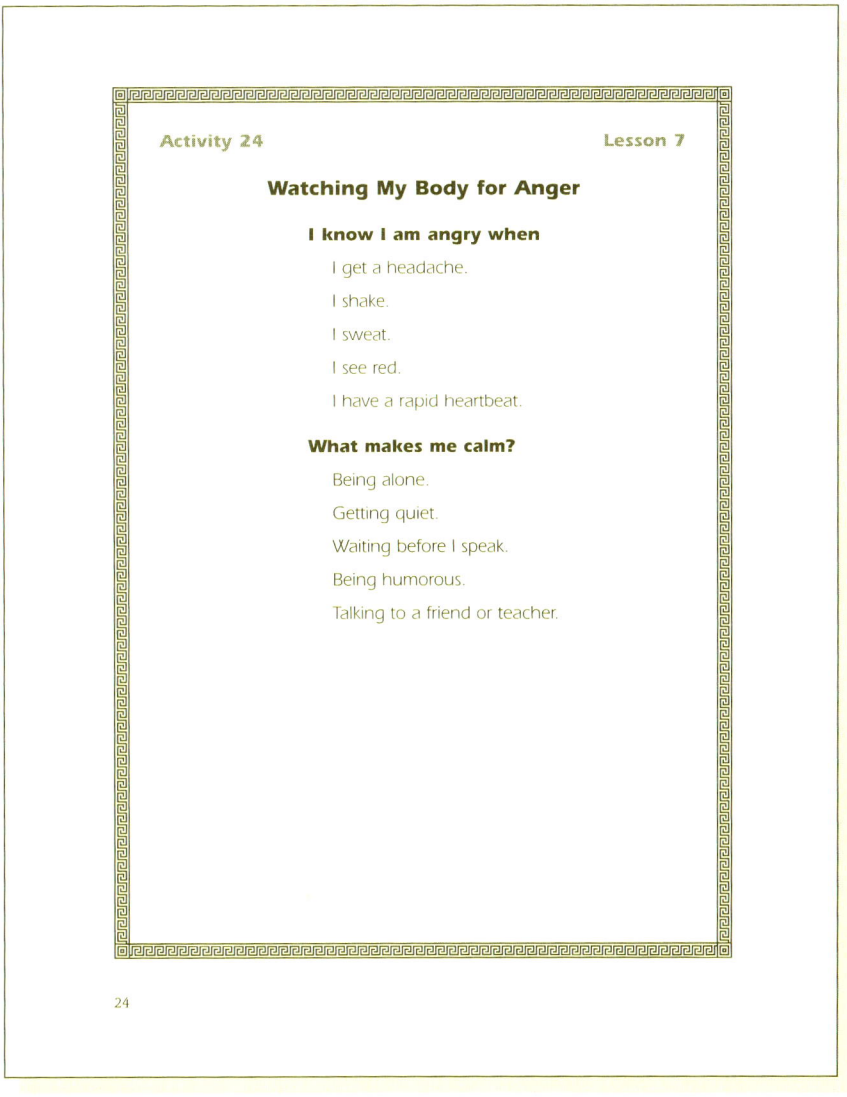

Activity 24 **Lesson 7**

Watching My Body for Anger

I know I am angry when

　I get a headache.

　I shake.

　I sweat.

　I see red.

　I have a rapid heartbeat.

What makes me calm?

　Being alone.

　Getting quiet.

　Waiting before I speak.

　Being humorous.

　Talking to a friend or teacher.

Student Manual
page 25

Activity 25   **Lesson 7**

What Should I Do When People Make Fun of Me?

I may choose to	What might happen	I choose to
Fight.	1. I could get hurt. 2. I can get in trouble.	
Make fun of them.	1. I might get in trouble. 2. People might believe I am not friendly.	
Not deal with it, cry, or run away.	1. The person bothering me might not stop. 2. I might not be happy with myself because I let myself be treated that way.	
Ignore it.	1. It might stop. 2. It might get worse first.	
Ask the person to stop by saying, "Do not speak to me that way."	1. I might feel good about myself. 2. The person might stop.	
Talk to a teacher.	1. The teacher may deal with the situation. 2. You can talk about your feelings.	

LESSON 7   **Pretest/Posttest**

Strategies for Handling Anger

Name _____ Date _____

Instructions: Read each sentence and check either **Yes** or **No.**

Yes **No**

❏ ❏ 1. I can think of a positive solution to a problem that usually makes me angry.

❏ ❏ 2. I know what events make me angry.

❏ ❏ 3. I am aware of my physical reactions when I become angry.

❏ ❏ 4. I know how I usually respond when I am angry.

❏ ❏ 5. I know what calms me down when I am angry.

☐ ☐ **Total**

LESSON 8

Dealing with My Emotions

GOAL To help students learn to identify and deal with the emotions they experience that are related to their disability

PROCEDURE
1. Review students' homework.

2. Administer the pretest.

3. Tell the class that emotions are universal and that they differ from person to person and situation to situation.

4. Remind students that because they have a disability in learning, they are bound to have emotions that run the gamut from exhilaration to sadness to frustration to tension to depression to guilt—many of them brought on by themselves as well as by others. Ask the class to share situations in which they have felt any of these types of emotions.

   As students discuss, they will begin to feel comfortable and, as a result, free to offer many examples of situations they have found emotionally wrenching or—on the bright side—emotionally uplifting.

   Although some students will have experienced positive emotions, many will report negative incidents related to their disability that left them feeling blue.

   A number of students will discuss feeling anxious about homework assignments, especially difficult assignments that require them to put in more effort than general education students.

   Anxiety may also result from students' feeling that they have disappointed their parents or teachers by failing to meet their expectations. In addition, they may be wrestling with negative emotions emanating from failure to meet their own goals.

5. Ask the class how they respond to their array of negative emotions.

   Some students will say that they fall into a state of depression because they feel helpless to resolve their problems. The anger they feel toward themselves and others, combined with their frustrations over their disability, can manifest itself as depression.

6. Ask students what happens when they respond to negative emotions.

   Students who become depressed tend to say that their sadness and depression only worsen. Some of them despair and give up hope completely.

7. Delving deeper, ask students whether they are aware of how they respond to different negative emotions.

   Most students will say they are aware that they "feel bad" but don't know what they need to do to "feel good."

8. Ask students how they can tell when they are becoming depressed or unhappy or guilty.

   Some students will recognize recurrent physical symptoms and, as a result, will not feel like getting out of bed in the morning.

   Other students will be aware of their emotions when they realize that they hate attending school.

   Still others will recognize their emotional plight when they notice that they are crying a lot and becoming angry over minor matters.

9. Ask the class how they are able to find some peace of mind in the face of such negativity.

   Students will most likely name activities such as playing sports, listening to music, and visiting with friends.

10. Have students turn to **Activity 26—Dealing with My Emotions—** on **page 26** of the Student Manual and help them review the definitions of the emotions described in the activity. Ask students to think about situations in which they have felt these emotions—either at school, home, or work—and to list on the page those situations and the ways students responded to them.

11. Remind students that everyone responds or reacts differently to emotions: sometimes negatively, sometimes positively. Whatever their response, it will be either harmful or helpful to them.

12. Tell students that their disability in learning can make them feel less valuable than others—that it can saddle them with a poor self-concept. Explain that in order to improve their self-concept, students may seek to accomplish something they feel is valuable to themselves and to others. By having fun with new hobbies (e.g., crossword puzzles or gardening or sports) and by doing volunteer work in the community, students will improve their self-concept and pave the way toward self-determination.

13. Ask the class to think of ways they can improve their self-concept. Following are a few suggestions by students:

    "I'd like to find some ways, some strategies that might help me complete my assignments at school without so much stress."

    "I need to figure out ways to keep my parents from worrying that my disability in learning will hamper my success."

    "As I work to improve in my areas of weakness, I also find myself improving in areas that I consider my strengths."

14. Encourage students to respond positively to their emotions. Have them turn to **Activity 27—Making Me Feel Better—**on **page 27** of the Student Manual, where they will have an opportunity to list activities that make them feel better.

15. Ask students how they can respond positively to a situation that might cause stress, frustration, depression, or guilt.

    At this juncture, students should be better able than before to think of positive ways to divert their attention from a negative situation and suggest alternatives that will enable them to relax. Suggestions might include participating in sports, helping out at home, doing something with a friend, going to a movie, listening to music, and so on.

16. Give students the following scenario:

    You stayed up late last night working on an assignment and really tried your best. You turned in the assignment on time but were soon disappointed when your teacher gave you a very low grade. Crestfallen, you felt like giving up. What should you have done at the time, or what should you do now?

    One idea suggested by students is to talk to the teacher and ask if you can resubmit the assignment.

    Another suggestion is to find someone—possibly a tutor—who can help you with future assignments.

17. Have students discuss and role-play several situations in which they have found themselves during the past week in school. Encourage them to continue to try to learn new strategies to improve their study skills.

18. Tell students that as they learn new strategies, they should keep in mind the need to think of positive responses to their emotions. By being positive, they will find it much easier to discover effective learning strategies.

19. Give the class a specific homework assignment, individualized for each student, and have them complete it before the next session.

20. Administer the posttest.

Student Manual
page 26

Activity 26   **Lesson 8**

Dealing with My Emotions

Emotion	Situation	Response
Depression		
Guilt		
Frustration		
Stress		

Student Manual
page 27

Activity 27   **Lesson 8**

Making Me Feel Better

Activities that make me feel better

1. _____
   _____
   _____

2. _____
   _____
   _____

3. _____
   _____
   _____

4. _____
   _____
   _____

5. _____
   _____
   _____

Lesson 8 • Dealing with My Emotions

Lesson 8 **Pretest/Posttest**

Dealing with My Emotions

Name _____ Date _____

Instructions: Read each sentence and check either **Yes** or **No**.

Yes **No**

☐ ☐ 1. I know how to make myself feel better when I have negative emotions.

☐ ☐ 2. I know what situations add to negative emotions.

☐ ☐ 3. I know how to respond in a positive way whenever I experience negative emotions.

☐ ☐ 4. Everyone experiences negative emotions.

☐ ☐ 5. It is OK for me to have negative emotions.

☐ ☐ **Total**

Lesson 9

Accepting Myself

GOAL For students to understand the significance of positive self-talk as they strive to accept themselves for who they are

PROCEDURE
1. Review students' homework.

2. Administer the pretest.

3. Explain to students that, although we may not realize it, we all send messages to ourselves every day—messages we refer to as self-talk. When we do something, whatever that something may be, our minds silently tell us whether what we did was good or bad, right or wrong, positive or negative, necessary or unnecessary, and so on.

4. Emphasize to the class that self-talk is either positive or negative.

5. To illuminate this point, discuss a normal, everyday occurrence, and then offer examples of the negative and positive self-talk that might follow. Students will probably recognize themselves as they notice the differences between these two types of self-talk.

   Scenario: You have just dropped and broken a glass that you were reaching for in the kitchen cupboard. Even though you may not say anything out loud, your mind will send you a message that you will silently say to yourself.

   Example of negative self-talk: "Wow, I sure am clumsy."

   Example of positive self-talk: "I made a mistake and broke the glass; I'll sweep the glass into a dustpan and try not to cut myself."

6. Have students turn to **Activity 28—Negative Messages—**on **page 28** of the Student Manual, which lists common negative messages that people "hear" as self-talk.

7. Ask students if they ever hear any of the messages presented in the activity.

   Although there will be variations among the specific messages students hear, they will answer with a resounding "yes."

8. Have students think of negative messages they send themselves every day in the form of negative self-talk. Engage them in a discussion that focuses on the reasons for their negative self-talk, such as failure to complete an assignment or an inability to pay attention in

class. Encourage students to think really hard about what it is that usually provokes their negative messages.

9. Students are likely to engage in negative self-talk. Ask them to describe some of the situations at school, at home, and in the community.

   In school, the problems usually center on difficulty with certain academic subjects. But problems also crop up when students try to socialize with their peers, yet are made to feel uncomfortable by students who would rather they not be part of the crowd. Because some peers make fun of their disability in learning, these students may feel they are correct when they engage in negative self-talk.

   At home, in addition to sending themselves negative messages because of conflicts with their parents, children and adolescents also think negative thoughts because of quarrels with siblings. They may feel, for instance, that Mom or Dad favors a brother or sister—even though there really is no evidence to support what has become simply negative self-talk.

   In the workplace or the community at large, students may subconsciously employ negative self-talk because of fear of failure to complete tasks, fear that their employer will find that they have a disability in learning and therefore are not capable of learning how to perform tasks, or fear that they will always be stuck in a low-paying job. Again, their discomfort is caused by what they are telling themselves, not what others are telling them.

10. To help students defeat their negative self-talk, suggest methods they can use to refute the negative messages that are swirling inside their heads. Tell students that each time they hear such a message in their mind, they need to reprogram their mind with positive thoughts. Whenever the negative message appears in their mind, they should immediately send themselves a positive message. They should then continue substituting positive self-talk for negative self-talk until the negative message no longer enters their mind.

11. Have students look at **Activity 29—Understanding My Self-Talk**—on **page 29** of the Student Manual. This activity discusses the concept of self-talk and gives examples of negative self-talk and positive self-talk.

12. Ask students to turn to **Activity 30—Self-Talk**—on **page 30** of the Student Manual. For each environment—school, home, and work—ask students to list the negative messages they send themselves most often. Then have them refute each negative message by listing opposite each one a positive message. Seeing the messages in writing will help students as they practice positive self-talk.

13. Read the following scenario to the class:

    Rhonda has a disability in learning. She is employed at the small grocery store on the corner and is responsible for working the checkout counter. Once in a while, the electronic checkout system shuts down, and Rhonda must check out customers manually. She says to herself, "I am very slow at making change for the customers. They must think I am dumb."

14. Ask students to come up with examples of positive self-talk that Rhonda can use to counter her negative self-talk. Following are likely student responses:

    "I am friendly and nice to the customers, and that is more important than giving them back their change quickly when the checkout system is broken."

    "I can ask the customers to be patient with me because the checkout system is broken, and it may take me a little more time than usual to check them out."

    "I think the customers will understand. Most people understand that when a job has to be done manually, it takes more time than it would with the help of a machine."

15. Ask the class to think about the following comment by a frustrated student with a disability in learning:

    "I have to work two or three times harder than other students just to get a C. It doesn't seem fair at all. I just feel like giving up."

16. Invite students to refute this negative self-talk with a positive message. A likely response would be something like this:

    "I have a disability in learning, and most people do not. I am passing in my class, though, and that is a very good sign. After all, I am doing my best."

17. Give the class a specific homework assignment, individualized for each student, and have them complete it before the next session.

18. Administer the posttest.

Student Manual
page 28

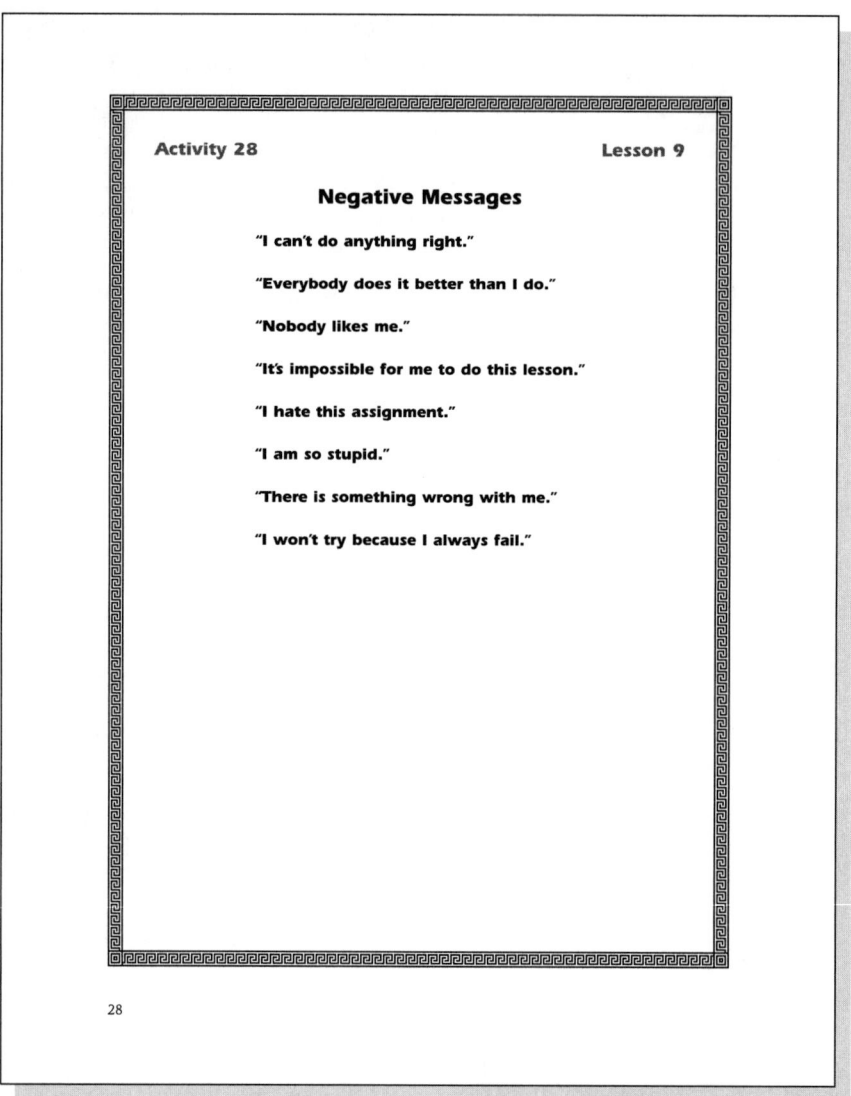

Activity 28 **Lesson 9**

Negative Messages

"I can't do anything right."

"Everybody does it better than I do."

"Nobody likes me."

"It's impossible for me to do this lesson."

"I hate this assignment."

"I am so stupid."

"There is something wrong with me."

"I won't try because I always fail."

Student Manual
page 29

Activity 29 **Lesson 9**

Understanding My Self-Talk

The brain controls and processes our feelings. We program our minds to think a certain way with our self-talk. We program ourselves by what we feel.

As our self-talk changes, our attitudes and the way we think change with our behavior.

Examples

Negative self-talk	Positive self-talk
"I can't do anything right."	"I am able to do most things right."
"Everybody does it better than I do."	"I am just as capable as others."
"I'm so clumsy."	"I have good coordination."
"I hate going to school."	"I learn a lot at school."
"My classmates hate me."	"I'm good at making friends."

Student Manual
page 30

Activity 30 **Lesson 9**

Self-Talk

Negative Self-Talk	Positive Self-Talk

School

1. _____ 1. _____
   _____   _____

2. _____ 2. _____
   _____   _____

Home

1. _____ 1. _____
   _____   _____

2. _____ 2. _____
   _____   _____

Work

1. _____ 1. _____
   _____   _____

2. _____ 2. _____
   _____   _____

LESSON 9   **Pretest/Posttest**

Accepting Myself

Name _____ Date _____

Instructions: Read each sentence and check either **Yes** or **No**.

Yes	No	
☐	☐	1. I know the meaning of self-talk.
☐	☐	2. I know the negative messages that I send to myself.
☐	☐	3. I know how to use positive self-talk to replace negative messages that I send to myself.
☐	☐	4. I know which negative messages are related to school, which to home, and which to work.
☐	☐	5. I know how to reprogram my mind to think positive rather than negative thoughts.
☐	☐	**Total**

Lesson 10

Making Friends and Getting Along with Others

GOAL For students to learn the keys to making friends and getting along with others

PROCEDURE
1. Review students' homework.

2. Administer the pretest.

3. Have the class turn to **Activity 31—Keys to Getting Along with Others**—on **page 31** of the Student Manual. Introduce them to and discuss the five essential keys to getting along with others: (a) listen, (b) be positive, (c) share, (d) value yourself, and (e) apologize.

4. Ask students to pause for a moment and think about their relationships with their friends, parents, teachers, and others. Then ask them whether they honestly pay attention to these people.

    Many students will reply that they do pay attention. Some, however, will have trouble accepting the premise of this question, maintaining that they have more problems than their friends without disabilities and thus may need more attention than their friends.

5. Try to bring the matter more clearly into focus by explaining to the class that everybody has problems in various areas and wants and needs attention, too—not just those who have a disability in learning. Then ask students whether they pay close attention to what others are saying, or whether they try to talk when others are telling their story. In other words, are the students actually listening to what others are saying?

    A couple of typical responses might be, "I try to listen to my friends when they talk" or "Sometimes I compare what is happening to me with what is happening to them."

    Emphasize that, although it is good to sympathize or celebrate with a person who is describing a situation, in actuality that person wants to tell his or her story uninterrupted. The person wants a listener who pays full attention.

6. Explain that everyone wants to be heard and enjoys being heard. Ask students to put themselves in someone else's shoes: Would they want the other person to listen to them?

7. Point out that careful listening is commonly referred to as "active listening." Tell the class that after listening to someone's story, they should be able to repeat back to the speaker what the speaker said.

8. Give students pointers on how to listen to a person. For example, tell them that they should look at the speaker, nod their head in agreement as they follow along, and occasionally say, "Uh-huh." These cues will tell the speaker that the listener is actively involved in communicating.

9. Ask students how they would initiate a conversation with someone.

    Most students will have little difficulty coming up with "Hello, how are you?"

10. Have students think about and share with the class some topics they might discuss with another person that would highlight their own positive qualities.

    Expect students to mention subjects in which they are doing well, such as art, music, math, English, history, and so on. The conversation may even get around to sports and other extracurricular activities.

11. Tell the class that all people tend to like others who view them in a positive light. Therefore, it is important to limit wisecracks and teasing when listening to someone talk. Even though the comments are most likely being made in jest, the other person might take the needling seriously and feel sad or alienated.

12. Make sure you get across to students the message that it is demeaning to people to hear harsh criticism, especially if they're simply talking about their school work or their activities or their likes and dislikes. Emphasize as well that students should take care not to be overly critical of themselves. Being rough on oneself opens the door to negative self-talk.

13. Have students answer the following questions and then discuss them with fellow classmates:

    Do you offer help to others when they need it?

    Are you always willing to do a favor for a friend?

    Do you tend to concentrate on yourself most or all of the time?

14. As the class discusses the answers to these questions, have them think of ways to help other people.

    Students will likely suggest doing chores around the house, helping the elderly in the neighborhood with lawn work or shopping, and being willing to alter their schedules so they can help others meet their needs.

15. Ask students what types of things are treasured in our culture.

    Some students will mention items of value such as money, cars, jewelry, houses, and other material things. Some will feel that friends and family are to be treasured and thus are valuable "commodities" that carry no price tag. Still others will maintain that if everybody owns these items, then they are not really valuable.

Remind students that different people treasure different things. Point out that listening to others and having others listen to them is extremely valuable and that once they have learned to communicate with and get along with others in harmony, they will have opened a veritable treasure chest.

16. Learning how to value others as well as oneself will enable students to recognize situations in which people are mistreated or shown a lack of respect. Ask students to recall incidents in which fellow students tagged along with others in hopes of being accepted by their group. These followers were mistreated but put up with the embarrassment anyway. Ask students for their comments.

    Most students have observed this phenomenon and will respond with a comment such as "These kids were being treated badly. Most of the time, the people they were following around said or did anything to them they wanted to."

17. Explain to students that if they value themselves, they won't let others mistreat them. Make sure they understand the importance of treating others as they would like to be treated and the need for them to apologize to someone if they hurt that person's feeling. Likewise, they should insist that a person who mistreated them apologize. Sometimes people feel the need to exact revenge for something someone has done to them. Explain that getting back at someone does nothing but vent anger and that anger is counterproductive; it may prove more harmful to the injured than to the culprit.

18. Ask for volunteers or select pairs of students to engage in a role play, with one student doing the talking and the other doing the listening. Have the listener repeat to the speaker what the speaker just said. Encourage everyone in the class to join in by pairing up with a classmate.

19. Have students turn to **Activity 32—Situational Analysis**—on **page 32** of the Student Manual. Ask them to choose a partner and then role-play one or more of the situations, or vignettes, presented in the first column of the activity. Next, have them write in column two their suggestions for better behavior.

    As students proceed with the activity, they should be able to recognize the negative behavior described in each vignette. It should become apparent to them that people who brag, tattle on others, try to control others, or try to get their way all the time are people who exhibit poor friendship skills and probably have fewer friends than others.

20. In getting along with others, students should understand that circumstances arise that challenge their ability to do just that. Some students find that they have unwittingly hurt someone's feelings. Although they did not intend to hurt the person, they still are responsible for saying something such as "I'm sorry. I shouldn't have said that to you."

21. Tell the class that other difficult situations do not necessarily require an apology. They do, however, require making a decision—one that can be construed as either negative or positive, yet one that is the students' to make. These types of situations present students with predicaments that only they can resolve. The consequences of their decision may still require an explanation or an apology to a teacher, a parent, or a good friend. Read the following scenario to the class:

    > You come home from your after-school job, and you have a lot of homework to do. But you are told that your friend across the street has had a death in the family. Although you know that, owing to your disability in learning, your assignment will take at least two hours to complete, you nevertheless want to console your friend. How will you handle the situation?

    As they discuss the situation, students will offer a variety of solutions: Some may decide to help their friend and then get up earlier than usual the next morning to complete their assignment. Others may decide not to do their homework at all and then offer an explanation to their teacher the following day. A few students may decide to tend to their friend after they have completed their homework.

22. Do not criticize or judge your students, regardless of their answers. Keep in mind—and have your students keep in mind—that people's value systems differ. Therefore, different students will come up with different solutions.

23. Remind students that they will encounter a variety of situations—some quite awkward—that will call on them to make decisions. To get along well with others, they must be fair both to themselves and to others. They should thus commit to memory the five essential keys to finding and keeping friends: (a) listen, (b) be positive, (c) share, (d) value yourself, and (e) apologize.

24. Give the class a specific homework assignment, individualized for each student, and have them complete it before the next session.

25. Administer the posttest.

Student Manual
page 31

Activity 31　　　　　　　　　　　　　　　　　Lesson 10

Keys to Getting Along with Others

Listen
Listen to others when they are talking. Don't just wait for them to stop speaking so you can get your point across or tell your story. Listen hard enough to be able to repeat what they are saying to you.

Be positive
Say positive things about yourself and other people. Limit complaints and negative comments.

Share
Reasonably share what you have with others. Giving can be a pleasurable experience to the person who gives as well as the person who receives. Sharing also includes your time and effort.

Value yourself
Be friendly, but don't try to make others be your friend. Don't sell yourself short. You are valuable.

Apologize
Being able to apologize when you hurt someone's feelings shows strong character.

Lesson 10 • Making Friends and Getting Along with Others

Student Manual
page 32

Activity 32 **Lesson 10**

Situational Analysis

Situation

1. Nequa is very controlling. When she walks up to a group and they are playing a game, she wants them to stop and play what she wants to play. Sometimes other children hate to see her coming.

   What is a better behavior? _____
   _____

Situation

2. Most kids don't want Malik around. He watches what everyone does. If he thinks that they are doing something wrong, he reports it to the teacher.

   What is a better behavior? _____
   _____

Situation

3. Paul talks about himself all the time. He says he is smart and talks about where he goes to have fun and how great he looks in his clothes. While you are in the middle of a sentence, he will interrupt you and continue to talk about himself.

   What is a better behavior? _____
   _____

Situation

4. Maria keeps her desk and locker in a mess. Sometimes she does not change her clothes. Sometimes she bites her nails or picks her nose.

   What is a better behavior? _____
   _____

Situation

5. Ralph often curses and says very rude things to others. He sometimes calls people bad names and says things about them behind their backs.

   What is a better behavior? _____
   _____

LESSON 10   Pretest/Posttest

Making Friends and Getting Along with Others

Name _____ Date _____

Instructions: Read each sentence and check either **Yes** or **No.**

Yes   No

☐   ☐   1. I know the keys to getting along with others.

☐   ☐   2. I know how to listen to others.

☐   ☐   3. I know how to make friends.

☐   ☐   4. I am really good at starting conversations.

☐   ☐   5. I know how to apologize when I'm wrong.

☐   ☐   **Total**

Lesson 11

Communicating with Parents

GOAL To teach students how to advocate for themselves to their parents appropriately and successfully and, in the process, get closer to them

PROCEDURE
1. Review students' homework.

2. Administer the pretest.

3. Discuss with the class some of the challenges they face when their parents feel anxious or even angry about their seeming lack of initiative. Ask students what type of feedback their parents usually give them on their academic performance. Following are some typical examples of student responses to their parents' angst:

    "I agree with my parents that I need to buckle down and improve in my studies."

    "I'm doing the best I can. It's just that I get frustrated with my school work, especially when I'm trying to do my homework."

    "I feel like something under a microscope. If I do poorly on my assignments, I feel my parents' eyes on me. I feel so frustrated because I can't really explain to them that it's not a matter of being lazy—it's that I'm trying to overcome my disability in learning."

4. Ask students to think of ways they can better communicate with their parents and get positive results.

5. Refer students to **Activity 33—Dialoguing with Parents—**on **page 33** of the Student Manual and have them script an imaginary dialogue with their parents. Remind students that their parents have their best interests at heart and want to communicate with them and help them succeed.

6. To help students practice communicating with their parents, ask for volunteers to pair up with other students and for each pair to role-play a dialogue between themselves and their (mock) parents.

7. Inform students that rehearsing a typical dialogue with their parents either by themselves or in role plays with classmates—and actually engaging in dialogue with their parents as well—will also help them dialogue with other adults, many of whom will need to know about their disability in learning. With practice, students will feel more relaxed as they describe the characteristics of their disability.

8. Emphasize to students that their parents deserve their respect and, as such, expect their children to speak to them in a positive, neutral, nonthreatening tone of voice. Following are examples of questions and comments you can encourage students to bring to the attention of their parents:

    "May I have your permission to sit down and talk with you about your concerns as well as mine? Maybe we can both learn something new about my disability in learning."

    "I think it would work best for me to reserve some time specifically for study. I realize that there will be days when that's not possible, but I'd certainly like to try."

    "Did you know that I've been staying up late every night to complete my homework? Most of the other kids get theirs done a lot faster, but my disability is getting in the way. Sometimes it's hard to function the next day because I'm so sleepy."

9. Parents should realize that, just as they are tired and in need of rest after a hard day's work, so are their children. Encourage students to tell their parents in a calm, reasoned manner that they, too, need to relax because they do in fact work very hard in school.

10. Have students turn to **Activity 34—Guidelines and Sample Schedule**—on **page 34** of the Student Manual. Ask them to study the sample schedule and to follow the guidelines that are provided. Tell them that experience and practice will help them pick up some helpful tips on planning how to fill blocks of time so that their schedule suits their individual study needs.

11. Direct students to **Activity 35—Schedule Form**—on **page 35** of the Student Manual and have them fill in the blanks on the schedule form either by themselves or with the help of their parents. Although students can use the form as a guide to their activities during the current week, they can also—with your encouragement— use it to record their schedules for the upcoming week.

12. Remind the class that they will get the most out of these activities if they include their parents in the process, especially the process involved in the scheduling strategy. Inform students that they should begin to feel a sense of control over their day-to-day activities. Tell them that this control will eventually enable them to move forward academically and strengthen their social skills with less parental monitoring.

13. It is vital that students always take their parents' thoughts and ideas seriously. In order to show parents that their children are working with them hand in hand, students should recall the good listening skills they learned in earlier lessons, stay focused, make suggestions rather than demands, and engage in active listening.

14. Active listening and a healthy give-and-take with adults are skills that students should polish every day. The following scenario is bound to ring a bell with many of your students.

Your English teacher has assigned you a seven-page paper that is due in two days. Because you have a problem with reading and writing, you feel nervous, pressured, and unsure of yourself.

15. Ask students to come up with ways to handle this problematic situation and share them with the class. Student responses might include the following:

    "Explain to the teacher that you have a disability in learning and describe its characteristics."

    "Tell the teacher that it usually takes you a long time to finish your assignments because of your difficulty in writing."

    "Ask the teacher if she can cut back your assignment to four or five pages instead of seven. Also ask if your deadline can be extended to three days instead of two."

    "Assure the teacher that you want to do a good job on the assignment. Tell her you're not trying to dodge your responsibilities but simply need some extra help."

16. Tell the class that if they are having difficulty convincing their English teacher of their disability, perhaps they can enlist the help of the special education teacher or even their parents. These adults may be better able to explain the situation to the teacher, who is accustomed to assigning homework without taking into consideration students who have disabilities in learning.

17. Your students should begin to feel more comfortable explaining what they need. Consequently, they will become more skillful in advocating for themselves.

18. Remind students that many of their school- and job-related problems can be minimized by communicating openly with their parents. Although teachers care about their students, parents obviously have a far greater stake in their children's education and social skills.

19. Give the class a specific homework assignment, individualized for each student, and have them complete it before the next session.

20. Administer the posttest.

Student Manual
page 33

Activity 33 **Lesson 11**

Dialoguing with Parents

Practice writing what you might say to your parents and what they might say in response. Choose whatever topic you wish.

I will say: **My parents will then say:**
_____ _____
_____ _____
_____ _____
_____ _____
_____ _____

I will say: **My parents will then say:**
_____ _____
_____ _____
_____ _____
_____ _____
_____ _____

I will say: **My parents will then say:**
_____ _____
_____ _____
_____ _____
_____ _____
_____ _____

Student Manual
page 34

Activity 34 **Lesson 11**

Guidelines and Sample Schedule

Guidelines

Plan your schedule so that you study about the same time every day.

Each day before studying, make a list of what needs to be accomplished so that you can focus more clearly on each task.

Use the first five minutes of each study session to review concepts you have already learned.

Study in one-hour blocks unless you need more time to complete a particular assignment.

Determine the order in which you will complete your assignments. (Hint: It's usually best to work on the most difficult or time-consuming assignment first so you can get the hard part out of the way and feel more relaxed as you continue.)

Take regularly scheduled breaks while studying.

Sample Schedule

Time	Mon	Tues	Wed	Thurs	Fri	Sat	Sun
4:00	home-work	home-work	home-work	home-work	TV	read	read
5:00	TV	play video	work on report	gym	relax with friends	chores	eat
6:00	eat	eat	work on report	eat	relax with friends	eat	TV
7:00	study math	study reading	eat	TV	relax with friends	read	study
8:00	TV	TV	library report	TV	relax with friends	TV	study
9:00	study reading	sleep	library report	sleep	relax with friends	TV	study
10:00	sleep	sleep	sleep	sleep	sleep	sleep	sleep

Lesson 11 • Communicating with Parents

Student Manual
page 35

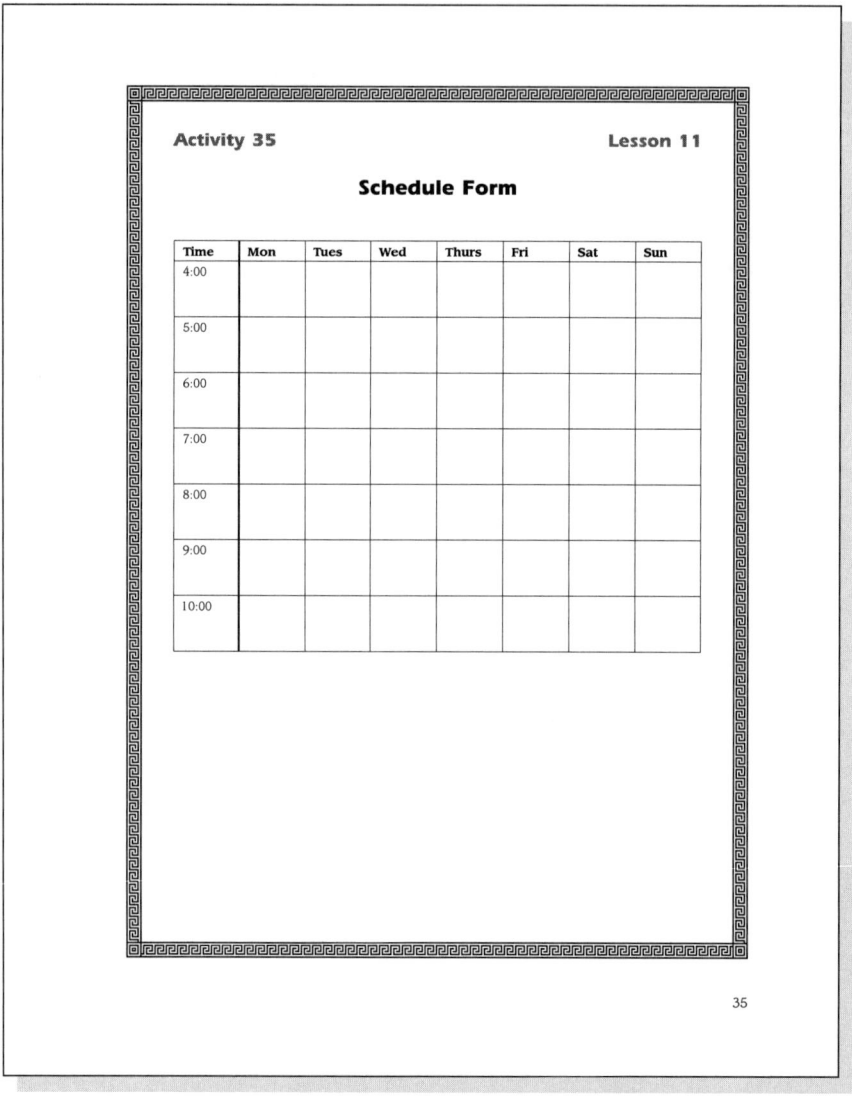

LESSON 11 Pretest/Posttest

Communicating with Parents

Name _____ Date _____

Instructions: Read each sentence and check either **Yes** or **No**.

Yes **No**

- ❏ ❏ 1. My parents understand why it may take me longer to do my work than it does others.
- ❏ ❏ 2. I know how to schedule my study time properly.
- ❏ ❏ 3. I have good communication skills with my parents.
- ❏ ❏ 4. I can explain my disability to my parents and my teachers.
- ❏ ❏ 5. My parents understand that I need time for rest and relaxation after school.

☐ ☐ **Total**

Lesson 12

Responsibility Basics

GOAL For students to learn the difference between responsible and irresponsible behavior and the importance of being responsible

PROCEDURE
1. Review students' homework.

2. Administer the pretest.

3. Ask the class to define the word *responsibility.*

    Most will understand that it means they must do what they promise to do—that they are obligated to complete homework assignments, help out with chores around the house, and be reliable at work.

4. Explain to students that responsibilities are activities and actions for which everyone is liable and accountable. Tell them that they have a responsibility to follow through on commitments to others, such as their teacher and classmates, parents, siblings, and employers.

5. Have students describe the responsibilities they have to themselves.

    Typical answers will dwell on the need for maintaining good personal grooming habits, getting good grades in school, completing chores at home, and showing up for work on time.

6. Ask students to describe the responsibilities they have to others.

    By now, most of the class will be aware that being responsible to others is contingent on their being responsible to themselves. In other words, by acting responsibly to themselves, they are simultaneously being responsible to others.

7. Refer students to **Activity 36—Responsibility—**on **page 36** of the Student Manual. As the class follows along, read the vignette and then ask students to answer the three questions that appear below the vignette.

8. Ask the class how they feel about responsibilities.

    Even after reading the vignette, some students will have a negative feeling about responsibilities. Most of the class, however, will understand the importance of being responsible.

9. Ask students to name some of the responsibilities they have in the classroom.

Typical responses will include listening to the teacher, following class rules, doing in-class assignments, and completing homework assignments.

10. Ask students what they don't like about classroom rules.

    To some students, classroom rules will seem a waste of time, restrictive, and an imposition.

    Most students (even some of those who feel constrained by certain regulations) will feel that classroom rules are an absolute necessity and that without rules, chaos will probably ensue.

11. Have the class turn to **Activity 37—Responsible or Irresponsible?**—on **page 37** of the Student Manual. After reading each scenario aloud, as the class follows along, ask students to decide what they would do in that particular situation and to write their solution on the activity page: Would they choose to engage in responsible behavior or irresponsible behavior? Why?

12. Ask students whether they are aware of how their responsible and irresponsible behaviors affect themselves and others. Open up the classroom to discussion.

13. Give the class a specific homework assignment, individualized for each student, and have them complete it before the next session.

14. Administer the posttest.

Student Manual
page 36

Activity 36 **Lesson 12**

Responsibility

You are president of the school's outreach group. The current goal of the group is to prepare a scrapbook that explains the mission and history of the group and shows photographs of the students in action, helping out with school projects and community volunteer efforts. As president of the group, you have taken it upon yourself to collect all the pertinent material the group has compiled and produce an attractive scrapbook for an upcoming conference.

There's a snag, however. Even though you know you'll need to plan ahead in order to finish the project, you fail to take into account your family's plans to go on vacation next week—and that you won't be returning until three days before the conference. In all the excitement, you forget to plan ahead and then find that you have only those three days to complete the scrapbook. You put the scrapbook together, but it is poorly prepared, and it is obvious to the members of your group and others how shabby it looks.

1. What happens when we are not responsible?

2. What happens to our work when we do not prepare and plan?

3. How do you think the group felt about your performance as president?

Lesson 12 • Responsibility Basics

Student Manual
page 37

Activity 37   **Lesson 12**

Responsible or Irresponsible?

Scenario 1: You ask your parents if you can have a dog, and you promise them that you will feed, wash, and walk the dog. Your parents buy you the dog. For about two months, you keep your promise, but then you become negligent in your duties because you are getting tired of the responsibility. You "forget" to feed and wash the dog and take it out for a walk.

Your solution: _____
_____
_____

Scenario 2: You promised your friend David that you would go to a movie with him on Saturday. But the next time you look at the calendar, you notice that the movie is showing at the same time as the community cleanup project. As president of the outreach group, you have already promised that you and your group would work on the project. Now, you don't want to help with the project.

Your solution: _____
_____
_____

Scenario 3: You want to be a pharmacist, and you have the ability to pursue this profession. However, you're not in the habit of completing your class work and homework and generally are not motivated to endure a tough course of study.

Your solution: _____
_____
_____

Scenario 4: You borrowed Natalie's gym shoes and promised her that you would not play basketball in them. Nonetheless, you go ahead and play basketball while wearing her shoes, and the shoes become scuffed and worn.

Your solution: _____
_____
_____

LESSON 12   **Pretest/Posttest**

Responsibility Basics

Name _____ Date _____

Instructions: Read each sentence and check either **Yes** or **No.**

Yes   **No**

- ❏ ❏   1. I know what responsible behavior means.
- ❏ ❏   2. I understand my responsibilities to others at school, home, and work.
- ❏ ❏   3. I understand my responsibilities to myself.
- ❏ ❏   4. I know what people think of me when I am irresponsible.
- ❏ ❏   5. I know the importance of following classroom rules.

☐ ☐   **Total**

Lesson 13

Paying Attention, Focusing, and Organizing

GOAL For students to learn strategies that will help them pay attention, stay focused, and build their organizational skills

PROCEDURE
1. Review students' homework.

2. Administer the pretest.

3. Ask the class the following questions and how they would answer them:

    Do you have difficulty paying attention and focusing?

    Do you have difficulty with organization?

    Where do you have the most difficulty paying attention and focusing? At school? Home? Work?

    Where do you have the most difficulty keeping organized? At school? Home? Work?

4. As students ponder their answers to these questions, refer them to **Activity 38—Strategies to Strengthen Focusing Skills**—on **page 38** of the Student Manual. There they will find a list of strategies intended to help them stay focused on classroom assignments and activities as well as out-of-class assignments they must complete at home or at the library. This list is especially helpful to students with disabilities in learning and should be kept nearby.

5. Have students turn to **Activity 39—Strategies to Strengthen Organizational Skills**—on **page 39** of the Student Manual. The activity also provides an invaluable set of strategies that students with disabilities in learning can use to help them strengthen their organizational skills. Have the class look these strategies over carefully and keep them handy.

6. Refer the class to **Activity 40—Strategies to Strengthen My Skills**—on **page 40** of the Student Manual. In this activity, have students list in one column the skills they feel they need to strengthen, and in the opposite column, the strategies they plan to use to strengthen these skills. In the end, each skill should be matched with a strategy intended to strengthen that specific skill.

7. Direct students to **Activity 41—Scheduling Tasks**—on **page 41** of the Student Manual and instruct them to use it as an aid in their scheduling of tasks.

8. Engage the class in some role playing. Read aloud the following three scenarios, or dilemmas, and have students either role-play their own thought patterns or role-play with classmates. Students should listen to the first scenario, engage in role play, and repeat the process for the next two scenarios.

    Scenario 1: You find yourself with some free time. Even though you have a paper due in five days, you are torn between watching TV and writing the paper. Which will you do? (Note: By now, students will have learned organizational strategies and the behaviors expected of them by parents and teachers.)

    Scenario 2: You have some outside chores to do at home this weekend, including mowing the lawn, trimming the hedges, and painting window frames. You also need to polish the paper you wrote that's due on Monday. How will you schedule your tasks?

    Scenario 3: You work at a mom-and-pop grocery store, stocking shelves and doing light cleaning. For the past couple of days, you've been sick. In the meantime, your work at the grocery store has piled up. When you return to work, you have to rearrange items on the shelves and then restock them with new merchandise that arrived with a shipment the previous day. What tool will you use to help you schedule your tasks? Try brainstorming with classmates and decide as a group how to tackle the problem.

9. Give the class a specific homework assignment, individualized for each student, and have them complete it before the next session.

10. Administer the posttest.

Student Manual
page 38

Activity 38 **Lesson 13**

Strategies to Strengthen Focusing Skills

In the classroom:

- Sit near the front of the class, close to the teacher.
- Do not sit in busy areas, such as near the classroom door, so you won't be interrupted by students' walking and chatting in the hallway.
- Try to join work groups composed of students who always complete their assignments. If you're having trouble with your class work, members of the work group and the teacher can assist you.

When doing your homework:

- Reserve a quiet space where you always do your homework.
- Before you begin each assignment, read the directions yourself or have your parents read the directions to you.
- Try to take a break every 15 minutes, using a timer to keep you on pace. Be sure to allow yourself enough time to complete the assignment.
- Try to do projects for your teachers to earn extra credit. At the least, try to think of extra-credit projects you can do at a later date.
- Make sure you give yourself a pat on the back for any improvements you make in strengthening your focusing skills.

Lesson 13 • Paying Attention, Focusing, and Organizing

Student Manual
page 39

Activity 39 **Lesson 13**

Strategies to Strengthen Organizational Skills

The following tips will help you stay organized:

- Always take enough time to organize yourself.
- Use a planner in which you can write all your assignments and the dates the assignments are due.
- Take time for daily planning. Make a list of assignments and duties for which you are responsible and begin the list with the most important (or the most difficult or time-consuming) task.
- Think ahead and plan your next week's schedule. If possible, try to plan your next month's schedule.
- As you read, use a fluorescent marker to highlight important parts of the text.
- Group similar tasks together and time yourself as you perform each task.
- Make sure you continue at a comfortable pace. Don't waste time or put tasks off for another day.
- Always set a specific deadline for long-term tasks.
- If possible, use a word processor for your assignments. It is faster and also safer because you can store your work on the computer's hard drive.

Student Manual
page 40

Activity 40 **Lesson 13**

Strategies to Strengthen My Skills

Skills That I Need to Strengthen	Strategies I Plan to Use to Strengthen My Skills
1.	
2.	
3.	
4.	
5.	
6.	
7.	
8.	
9.	
10.	

Lesson 13 • Paying Attention, Focusing, and Organizing

Student Manual
page 41

Activity 41 **Lesson 13**

Scheduling Tasks

Time	Task

LESSON 13   **Pretest/Posttest**

Paying Attention, Focusing, and Organizing

Name _____ Date _____

Instructions: Read each sentence and check either **Yes** or **No.**

Yes   **No**

- ❏   ❏   1. I need organizational skills.
- ❏   ❏   2. I know several organizational strategies.
- ❏   ❏   3. I need skills that will help me pay attention.
- ❏   ❏   4. I know several focusing strategies.
- ❏   ❏   5. I know how to plan, manage, and schedule tasks.

☐   ☐   **Total**

Lesson 14

Rejecting Discrimination

GOAL For students to recognize and reject discrimination in their everyday lives

PROCEDURE
1. Review students' homework.

2. Administer the pretest.

3. Spark a class discussion by asking students if they know what *discrimination* means.

4. While fielding students' responses, inform the class that *discrimination* is also commonly referred to as *bias* or *prejudice*. All three words are often used interchangeably. Ask students if they are familiar with these other two terms.

   Although some students will know that *discrimination* is another word for *bias* and *prejudice*, many others will not.

5. Explain to the class that discrimination, bias, and prejudice indicate a shunning of someone or some group. Those who practice discrimination assume (often subconsciously and always irrationally) that another person or group of people are "different" or inferior because of their ethnic background, skin color, religious preference, gender, or any other illogical reason.

6. Explain further that discrimination hurts because it attributes certain characteristics to people through the use of gross overgeneralizations. People with disabilities in learning are often regarded as abnormal by people who do not understand the disabilities.

7. Ask students if they have ever encountered discrimination and, if so, whether they remember how they felt about being labeled "slow" or "lazy" or "dumb"—especially considering that the name-caller had never before met or spoken with them.

   Students will be able to cite a goodly number of incidents in which they were spurned, dismissed, or laughed at by others because of their disability in learning. Some will also point out that people have discriminated against them and others for reasons that have nothing to do with a disability in learning.

8. Ask the class why they think people practice discrimination.

Opinions will vary, so introduce students to a well-known, inherently irrational reason for prejudice: People who are biased toward others tend to feel inferior themselves and therefore have a need to take out their frustrations on anyone they deem different. Unsure of their own capabilities and lacking in self-confidence, these people hurt others in order to feel superior. Their game is to build themselves up by tearing others down.

9. Ask the class to pause and take an honest look at their own views and behaviors: Do they practice discrimination themselves? Are they biased toward certain people and groups? If so, do students consider their own biases acceptable because they have been shunned and hurt in the past and therefore have an "excuse" for discriminating against others?

   It is here that students will tend to have trouble recognizing their own prejudices—if indeed they have them. They may believe that they do not have any prejudicial feelings at all. (It's not easy for anyone to own up to feelings of prejudice.) Consequently, it is up to you to help make them aware of any biases they might have and to coax them to recall how bad they feel when they encounter prejudice by others.

10. While students continue to think about discrimination and check their own prejudiced attitudes, ask them to voice their opinions. By sharing their experiences with the class, students will be better able to understand that discrimination—as damaging and irrational as it is—is practiced by nearly everybody at one time or another.

11. Have students turn to **Activity 42—Discriminatory Statements—** on **page 42** of the Student Manual. Ask them to read the discriminatory remarks in the left-hand column and explain why these comments are considered discriminatory, listing their reasons in the right-hand column.

12. Ask the class to take part in the following classroom exercise, which is intended to show them how ludicrous discrimination is and how unfair, insensitive, and damaging it is to all concerned:

    Separate students according to those who wear glasses and those who don't. Tell the class that the students who don't wear glasses will be able to spend the rest of the session drawing pictures and just taking it easy, whereas those who do wear glasses will be closely supervised and given a pop quiz before the bell rings.

    It won't take long before the entire class gets the point: that stereotyping people (or assigning certain traits to people for no logical reason) and prejudging them is senseless and has no basis in reality.

13. Explain to the class that discrimination is sometimes manifested in ways that at first glance seem to be normal or nondiscriminatory, but are in fact discriminatory. Read the following scenario to students and ask them to explain what part discrimination plays in it:

> Peter has been working at the same job for more than a year. On arriving at work Monday morning, he is told that government officials are checking the green cards of all Hispanic Americans. (The green card is an ID card. It is issued to immigrants to the United States so they can carry proof of their legal residency in this country.) What's confusing to Peter is that, although he is of Cuban heritage—and therefore Hispanic American—his immediate family and close relatives have been living and working in the United States for three generations.

  Discuss Peter's situation with the class. Give students ample opportunity to voice their opinions and talk about their own experiences, some of which might parallel Peter's.

14. Ask students if they feel they are now better equipped to spot signs of discrimination than they were before this lesson. Have them explain the ways discrimination affects people with disabilities in learning, people whose physical appearance is thought of as abnormal, or even people who are decent and kind and popular.

15. Give the class a specific homework assignment, individualized for each student, and have them complete it before the next session.

16. Administer the posttest.

Student Manual
page 42

Activity 42   **Lesson 14**

Discriminatory Statements

Explain in the right-hand column why the remarks in the left-hand column are discriminatory.

Discriminatory statement	Why is it discriminatory?
All Asian American women are obedient.	
Old people can't think. People's minds get slow when they get old.	
Women are not as proficient as men in math and science.	
I really hated it when those people moved into the neighborhood. They lowered our property value.	

Lesson 14 • Rejecting Discrimination

LESSON 14   Pretest/Posttest

Rejecting Discrimination

Name _____ Date _____

Instructions: Read each sentence and check either **Yes** or **No**.

Yes **No**

❏ ❏ 1. I know what discrimination means.

❏ ❏ 2. I know that discrimination, bias, and prejudice all mean the same thing.

❏ ❏ 3. I know why people discriminate against others.

❏ ❏ 4. People with disabilities are discriminated against.

❏ ❏ 5. I also discriminate at times.

☐ ☐ **Total**

LESSON 15

Getting a Job

GOAL To teach students the skills they will need in order to apply for and get a job

PROCEDURE
1. Review students' homework.

2. Administer the pretest.

3. Mention the word *independence* to the class and ask them what it means.

    The typical student response will be that independence represents freedom and therefore the opportunity to be on one's own.

4. Ask students if they are eager to get out on their own and whether independence for them will mean being able to do whatever they please.

    By a clear majority, students will be fired up at the thought of being independent. They will feel this way in part because they believe that if they are independent, they will be able to call their own shots and essentially do whatever they please.

5. Bring students back down to earth by reminding them of the lessons they learned earlier about responsibility. Explain to them that if they fancy the freedom that independence brings, they will have to use that freedom responsibly, for their actions affect others. Once they graduate and become members of the larger community, they will encounter situations that require them to be responsible. Regardless of whether they act responsibly or irresponsibly, they will be held accountable.

6. Tell the class that there are all sorts of ways to exhibit independence and responsibility. Ask students to think of ways in which they display these two assets.

    Some students will mention responsible behaviors they have displayed in class or elsewhere in school—completing homework on time, behaving well in class, being nice to others, respecting teachers and administrators, and so on.

    Other students, thanks to your words of caution about the price of freedom, will begin to visualize themselves as adults doing grown-up things. They will note that they—not their parents—will be washing their own clothes, feeding themselves, finding a place to live, paying rent, and looking for employment.

7. Explain to students that getting a job is one of the surest ways for them to prove that they are mature and responsible. If they don't get a job, they will be hard-pressed to find food and shelter. If they get a job, perform well for their employer, and therefore keep their job, they will be able to care for themselves and at the same time be accountable to others.

   Students who are paying close attention will also think about the role that responsibility plays in marriage, child rearing, and community service and interaction.

8. Encourage students to ponder career possibilities. Remind them that acquiring a part-time, after-school job is the first step toward obtaining employment after graduation from school.

   Many students will want to talk about the different types of jobs they've had, how much they've earned, and the differences between working a part-time job during school and a full-time job during the summer.

9. Even though most students will agree that it's a great feeling to receive a paycheck, be sure to put things in perspective. Although you should encourage students to find a job they like, you should urge them to be realistic about their earning potential. With few exceptions, students who have after-school jobs will not be making a lot of money—probably minimum wage. Therefore, it wouldn't make much sense for them to drop out of school; they do have extra money, but even if they were to put in a 40-hour work week, the money earned would probably be insufficient to support one person, let alone an entire family.

10. Assuming that your students plan to stay in school, let them know that their schoolwork comes first, that their jobs should never interfere with their lessons. Be blunt: Tell students that they should not even consider quitting school to go to work unless they absolutely must. (In some cases, you should note, family circumstances will force students to find full-time employment as soon as possible.)

    Some members of your class might balk at this warning, claiming that they're making a lot of money right now and aren't having any financial problems.

    Here is where you must remind students that (in most cases) they are living at home, not paying rent, not buying food, and probably not cooking meals, either. Were you to ask them whether, in all honesty, they feel they could get by—even prosper—in the world without benefit of all these freebies, they might feel differently about making an early exit from school.

11. Point out to students that getting a job is not all about making money; it's also about strengthening communication skills, learning how to open a checking or savings account, taking time for self-exploration (i.e., discovering which jobs are best suited to your abilities, interests, and temperament), and advocating for yourself en route to building self-determination skills.

12. Ask students what they have learned from having a job.

    Answers will vary, but most students will say they learned the necessity for showing up on time (or even a little early); being friendly and getting along with employers, co-workers, and customers; and doing the required work.

13. Ask students if they have fun working.

    Different students will come up with different responses. For each student who has fun on the job, there will be another student who finds his or her job unpleasant or the working conditions less than ideal.

14. Explain to the class that working a part-time job will help them learn how to manage their time and schedule their homework assignments. By focusing on their schedules, students will also be inclined to concentrate harder on their lessons. They will be in a groove.

15. By meeting the basic requirements—picking up an application and filling it out completely and cleanly, putting together an error-free résumé that highlights their strong points, dressing neatly and appropriately before going in for an interview, engaging in active listening during the interview, and exuding self-confidence—students will feel more self-assured than usual. In short, they will be exhibiting self-regulated and goal-directed behaviors. Make sure the class understands and appreciates the upside of the job-search process.

16. Let students know that you are aware that some of their parents don't think they are capable of holding down a job during the school year for fear it will interfere with their studies. If this is the case, encourage students to talk with their parents about the situation and remind their parents that working is a lot more constructive than some of the alternatives, such as watching TV or playing video games.

17. Ask students to come up with several modes of transportation they can use to get to work.

    Some students, having passed drivers' ed, will say they are able to drive to work (as long as their parents agree, and assuming they are not within walking distance of work), whereas others will say they either ride their bike or walk to work because they live close by.

18. Suggest to students that they learn how to use public transportation and have a friend or parent accompany them the first time: Students may need help counting the correct change to give to the bus driver; figuring out how to transfer to another bus, if necessary; and learning how to read the schedules. Another reason to rely on someone else's help is that they can point out landmarks that will indicate where the bus stop is.

19. As for students who don't yet have a job but are seeking employment, ask them the following questions:

Lesson 15 • Getting a Job

Do you have any job experience?

What experience do you have?

What type of job would you like to have?

How much time can you spend working?

Have you ever filled out a job application?

Do you know how to complete a résumé?

20. Have the class turn to **Activity 43—Sample Job Application**—on **page 43** of the Student Manual. Emphasize to students the importance of filling it out neatly. Suggest that they photocopy the application, answer the questions on a plain piece of writing paper, and then transfer their answers to the original application. Tell them that, most important, their answers must be truthful.

21. Ask students to turn to **Activity 44—Preparing a Résumé**—on **page 44** of the Student Manual. Tell them that you will help them complete their résumé so they can gain experience providing the necessary information. Make sure everyone in the class understands the importance of being honest when completing résumés and applications.

22. Have students turn to **Activity 45—Sample Interview Questions**—on **page 45** of the Student Manual and ask them if they are familiar with some of the interview questions listed on the page. Then ask the class to answer each question. Although they cannot possibly know exactly what type of questions a prospective employer might ask, most students who have interviewed for a job will have had to answer one or more of these questions.

23. After asking students how they should dress for an interview, have them turn to **Activity 46—Dressing Appropriately**—on **page 46** of the Student Manual. Here is where they can list or draw articles of clothing that are deemed appropriate to wear for an interview. Explain to students that, although they should look neat and well groomed for the interviewer, they should take into consideration the type of job for which they are applying and dress accordingly. For example, if they are applying for work at a fast-food restaurant, the interviewer may find it odd if a male applicant wears a coat and tie and a female applicant wears a fancy dress.

24. Point out to students that, just as they must be honest when answering interview questions, so must they be honest with their supervisor, fellow employees, and customers. How they act on the job will have a bearing on their future with their employer and, for that matter, other prospective employers who might find out about their current job performance. To spell it out, any person your students work for will be expecting them to possess the attributes listed in **Activity 47—Good Job Skills**—on **page 47** of the Student Manual. Have students review these attributes, read the scenario, and answer the questions.

25. Tell the class that the attributes that employers find desirable in their applicants are the same attributes that others find desirable. Therefore, students must learn to apply their positive traits to all environments—school, home, and work.

26. By now, students should be able to name the types of jobs for which they are best suited. Also, they should feel comfortable filling out applications, fashioning résumés, and answering interview questions. To help students and ensure that they understand the skills and attributes that are required of them, review with them the activities in this lesson. As you do, don't be surprised if students virtually overwhelm you with questions and suggestions, some of which will most likely tie in with earlier lessons.

27. To satisfy your curiosity and at the same time motivate students to brainstorm, ask those who have already had jobs whether this lesson taught them anything new (e.g., new strategies) that they can use when looking for another job.

28. Give the class a specific homework assignment, individualized for each student, and have them complete it before the next session.

29. Administer the posttest.

Student Manual
page 43

Activity 43 **Lesson 15**

Sample Job Application

First Name _____ Middle Initial ____ Last Name _____
Street Address _____ City _____ State ____ Zip _____
Home Phone Number _____ Emergency Phone Number _____
Social Security Number _____ Date of Birth _____
Person to be reached in case of an emergency:
Name _____ Relation _____

Previous Work Experience (beginning with most recent)

1. From _____ To _____
   Employer's Name, City, and Phone Number:
   _____
   _____
   _____

2. From _____ To _____
   Employer's Name, City, and Phone Number:
   _____
   _____
   _____

3. From _____ To _____
   Employer's Name, City, and Phone Number:
   _____
   _____
   _____

Education
School _____ Grade Level _____
Honors, Awards, and Skills: _____
_____
_____

Are you a U.S. citizen? ____ Yes ____ No

Student Manual
page 44

Activity 44 **Lesson 15**

Preparing a Résumé

Name _____
Address _____
Phone Number _____

Objective

_____
_____
_____
_____
_____
_____

Work Experience

_____
_____
_____
_____
_____
_____

Education

_____
_____
_____
_____
_____
_____

Student Manual
page 45

Activity 45   **Lesson 15**

Sample Interview Questions: How Would You Answer These?

Question	Answer
Why do you want to work for us?	
Have you had experience with the job for which you are applying?	
Have you ever been fired or quit a job? Why?	
Have you ever stolen something or been convicted of a crime?	
Why did you leave your previous job? What did you like most and least about it?	
What organizations do you belong to? What are your hobbies?	
What are your goals? For yourself? For the company?	
What is your educational level, and do you plan to continue school?	
Do you have transportation?	
Can you take constructive criticism?	

Student Manual
page 46

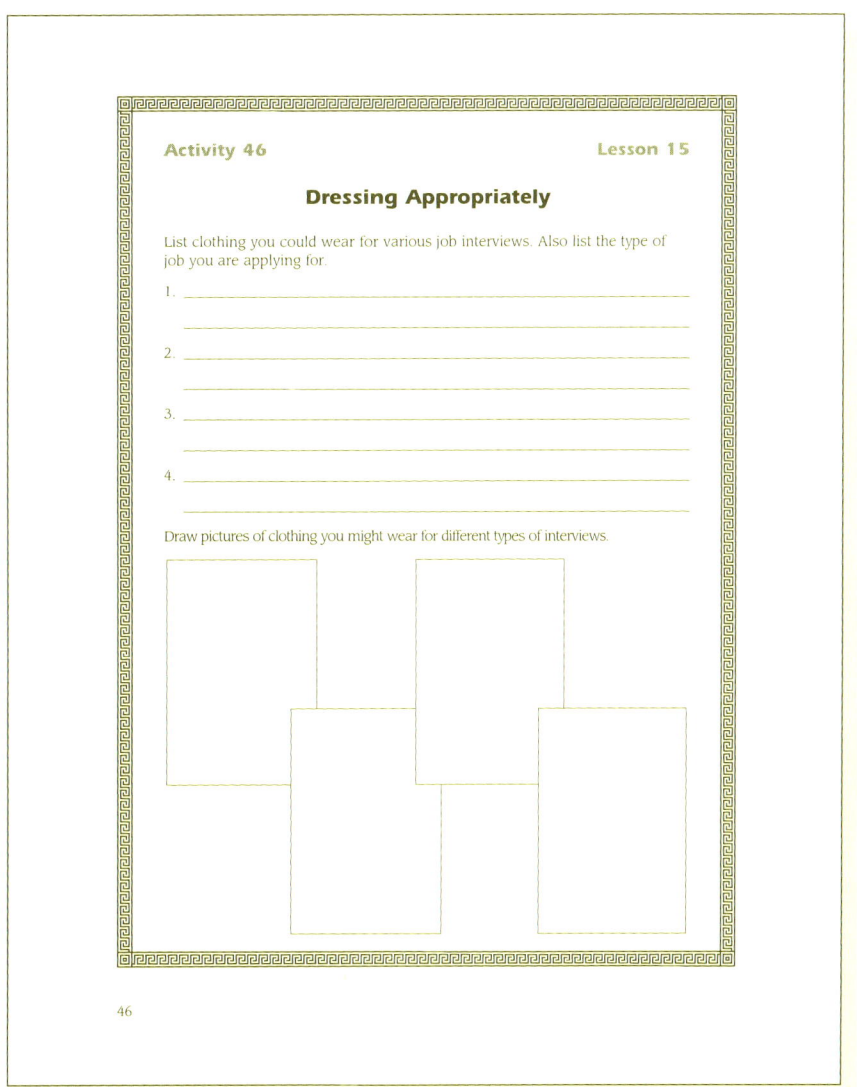

Student Manual
page 47

Activity 47 **Lesson 15**

Good Job Skills

You have good job skills when you are . . .

Dependable

Punctual

Neat

Social

Able to Follow Instructions

Cooperative

Respectful of Everyone

Read the following scenario. What work skill is Rashad missing? What good work skills does he have?

　Rashad leaves bright and early for work each day. He irons his clothes at night so that he won't have so much to do in the morning. He likes his job because he has many friends on the job. He talks to them at lunch and during break. Rashad likes everyone but his boss, about whom he frequently says, "He is always trying to tell me how to do my job. I know more about this job than he does. The next time he says something to me, I am going to let him know."

_____
_____
_____
_____
_____

LESSON 15 **Pretest/Posttest**

Getting a Job

Name _____ Date _____

Instructions: Read each sentence and check either **Yes** or **No**.

Yes **No**

❏ ❏ 1. I know what type of job I will be able to do well.

❏ ❏ 2. I know how to complete a job application.

❏ ❏ 3. I know what types of interview questions I will be asked when applying for a job.

❏ ❏ 4. I know the importance of good grooming when interviewing for a job.

❏ ❏ 5. I know the meaning of independence.

☐ ☐ **Total**

References and Resources

Amen, A. J., & Johnson, S. R. (1996). *A teenager's guide to ADD: Understanding and treating attention deficit disorders through the teenage years.* Fairfield, CA: Mindworks.

Argan, M., Snow, K., & Swaner, J. (1999). Teacher perceptions of self-determination: Benefits, characteristics, and strategies. *Education and Training in Mental Retardation and Developmental Disabilities, 34*(3), 293–301.

Campbell-Whatley, G. D. (1998). *The disability knowledge checklist survey.* Unpublished checklist.

Campbell-Whatley, G. D. (2001). Mentoring students with mild disabilities: The nuts and bolts of program development. *Intervention in School and Clinic, 36*(4), 211–216.

Cartledge, G., & Milburn, J. F. (1995). *Teaching social skills to children and youth: Innovative approaches.* Boston: Allyn & Bacon.

Cicci, R. (1995). *What's wrong with me? Learning disabilities at home and school.* Baltimore: York.

Cummings, R., & Fisher, G. (1993). *The survival guide for teenagers with learning differences.* Minneapolis, MN: Free Spirit.

Denison, K. (1996). *I wish I could fly like a bird!* Albany, NY: Fort Orange.

Dunn, K. B., & Dunn, A. B. (1993). *Trouble with school: A family story about learning disabilities.* Columbus, OH: Woodbine House.

Field, S. (1996). Self-determination instructional strategies for youth with disabilities. *Journal of Learning Disabilities, 29*(1), 40–52.

Field, S., & Hoffman, A. (1994). *Steps to self-determination.* Austin, TX: PRO-ED.

Field, S., Martin, J., Miller, R., Ward, M., & Wehmeyer, M. (1998). *A practical guide for teaching self-determination.* Reston, VA: Council for Exceptional Children.

Fisher, G. L., & Cummings, R. W. (1990). *The survival guide for kids with LD (learning differences).* Minneapolis, MN: Free Spirit.

Gehret, J. (1996). *The don't give up kid.* Fairport, NY: Verbal Images.

Gerber, P. J., Ginsberg, R., & Reiff, H. B. (1992). Identifying alterable patterns in employment in highly successful adults with learning disabilities. *Journal of Learning Disabilities, 24,* 475–487.

German, S. L., Martin, J. E., Marshall, L. H., & Sale, R. P. (2000). Promoting self-determination: Using "Take Action" to teach goal attainment. *Career Development for Exceptional Individuals, 23,* 27–38.

Giler, J. Z. (2000). *Socially adept: A manual for parents of children with ADHD and/or learning disabilities.* Santa Barbara, CA: CES Publications.

Goldstein, A. P., & McGinnis, F. (1997). *Skillstreaming the adolescent.* Champaign, IL: Research Press.

Gray, C. (2000). *The new social story book.* (Illustrated ed.). Arlington, TX: Future Horizons.

Harwell, J. M. (1989). *Complete learning disabilities handbook: Ready to use techniques for teaching learning handicapped students.* West, NY: The Center for Applied Research in Education.

Helper, N. M. (1955). Learning theory and self-concept. *Journal of Abnormal and Social Psychology, 5,* 184–194.

Jacobs, E. H. (1998). *Fathering the ADHD child: A book for fathers, mothers, and professionals.* Northvale, NJ: Jason Aronson.

Kent, K., & Quinlan, K. A. (1996). *Extraordinary people with disabilities.* Danbury, CT: Children's Press.

Levine, M. (1990). *Keeping ahead in school: A student's book about learning abilities and learning disorders.* Toronto, Ontario, Canada: Educators Publishing Service.

Levine, M. (1993). *All kinds of minds: A young student's book about learning abilities and learning disorders.* Cambridge, MA: Educators Publishing Service.

McGinnis, F., & Goldstein, A. P. (1997). *Skillstreaming the elementary school child.* Champaign, IL: Research Press.

Morganett, R. S. (1994). *Skills for living: Group counseling activities for elementary students.* Champaign, IL: Research Press.

Muller, D. (1978). *Self-concept: A new alternative for education.* The College of Education Dialogue Series Monograph. Las Cruces: New Mexico State University. (ERIC Document Reproduction Service No. ED165067)

Muller, D., Chambliss, J., & Muller, A. (1983, March). *Making self-concept a relevant education concern.* Paper presented at the annual conference of the Association for Supervision and Curriculum Development, Houston, TX.

Obiakor, F. E., Algozzine, B., & Campbell-Whatley, G. D. (1997). Self-concept assessment and intervention. *Australian Journal of Learning Disabilities, 1*(2), 17–22.

Parker, H. C. (1999). *Put yourself in their shoes: Understanding teenagers with attention deficit hyperactivity disorder.* Plantation, FL: Specialty Press.

Piers, E. V. (1996). *Piers-Harris Children's Self-Concept Scale*. Los Angeles: Western Psychological Services.

Roby, C. (1994). *When learning is tough: Kids talk about their learning disabilities*. Morton Grove, IL: Albert Whitman.

Rodis, P., Garrod, A., & Boscardin, M. L. (2001). *Learning disabilities and life stories*. Boston: Allyn & Bacon.

Rosner, J. (1993). *Helping children overcome learning disabilities* (3rd ed.). New York: Walker.

Silver, L. B. (1998). *The misunderstood child: Understanding and coping with your child's learning disabilities* (3rd ed.). New York: Random House.

Strichart, S. S., Mangrum, C. T., & Iannuzzi, P. (1998). *Teaching study skills and strategies to students with learning disabilities, attention deficit disorders, or special needs* (2nd ed.). Boston: Allyn & Bacon.

Taylor, J. (1994). *Hyperactive attention deficit child*. Rocklin, CA: Prima.

Wall, M. E., & Dattilo, J. (1995). Creating option rich learning environments: Facilitating self-determination. *Journal of Special Education, 29,* 276–294.

Wehman, P., & Kregel, J. (1997). *Functional curriculum for elementary, middle, and secondary age students with special needs*. Austin, TX: PRO-ED.

Wehmeyer, M., & Schwartz, M. (1997). Self-determination and positive adult outcomes: A follow-up study of youth with mental retardation and learning disabilities. *Exceptional Children, 63*(2), 245–256.

Wehmeyer, M. L., Argan, M., & Hughes, C. (2000). A national survey of teachers' promotion of self-determination and student-directed learning. *Journal of Special Education, 34*(2), 58–68.

West, M. D., Barcus, M., Brooke, V., & Rayfield, R. G. (1995). An exploration analysis of self-determination of persons with disabilities. *Journal of Vocational Rehabilitation, 5,* 357–364.

About the Author

Gloria D. Campbell-Whatley received her Ed.D. from the University of Alabama in Tuscaloosa. She is currently at the University of North Carolina at Charlotte, where she teaches doctoral- and master-level courses in special education. She has taught fourth grade and has been a special education teacher as well as a special education administrator.

Her research focuses on social skills and diversity issues in special education. She has written articles for various leading journals in her field, including *Intervention in School and Clinic* and *Teacher Education and Special Education.* She recently wrote *Strategies and Procedures in Designing Proactive Interventions with Culturally Diverse Populations with E/BD Children and Their Caregivers,* a title in the Council for Exceptional Children (CEC) Mini Library Series for the Council for Children with Behavior Disorders.

Dr. Campbell-Whatley has led research strands and preconference workshops for various divisions of CEC. In addition, she has led several workshops and presentations for various schools and communities and has made a number of juried research paper presentations at state, regional, national, and international conferences. She has been a guest lecturer at universities in Benin, West Africa, and Teresina, Brazil.

Dr. Campbell-Whatley was elected to the CEC Board of Directors in 2002 and has been an officer for several CEC chapters. She has also served as a proposal reviewer for several annual conferences, and she reviews manuscripts for *Teaching Exceptional Children* and *Teacher Education and Special Education.*